SOUTH BRITTANY

ADLARD COLES
Bloomsbury Publishing Plc
50 Bedford Square, London, WC1B 3DP, UK
29 Earlsfort Terrace, Dublin 2, Ireland

BLOOMSBURY, ADLARD COLES and
the Adlard Coles logo are trademarks of
Bloomsbury Publishing Plc

First published in Great Britain 2023

▼ Île d'Yeu, *page 134*

All internet addresses given in this book
were correct at the time of going to press.
The author and publisher regret any
inconvenience caused if addresses have
changed or sites have ceased to exist, but can
accept no responsibility for any such changes

A catalogue record for this book is available
from the British Library

Library of Congress Cataloguing-in-
Publication data has been applied for

ISBN: flexiback: 978-1-4729-8573-6; ePUB:
978-1-4729-8574-3; ePDF: 978-1-4729-8571-2

10 9 8 7 6 5 4 3 2 1

Typeset in Spectral and Source Sans
Designed by Austin Taylor
Printed and bound in India by
Replika Press Pvt Ltd

MIX
Paper from
responsible sources
FSC® C016779

To find out more about our authors and
books visit www.bloomsbury.com and
sign up for our newsletters

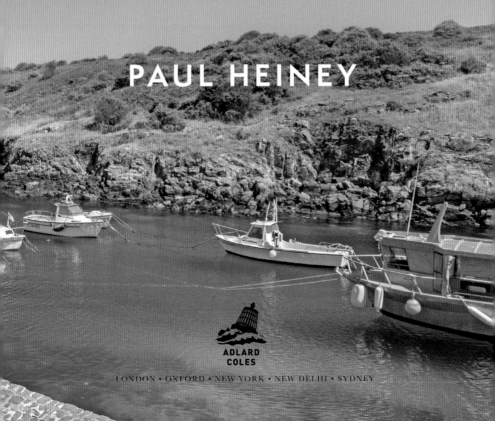

ADLARD
COLES
SHORE
GUIDE

SOUTH BRITTANY

Everything you need to know
when you step ashore

PAUL HEINEY

ADLARD
COLES

LONDON · OXFORD · NEW YORK · NEW DELHI · SYDNEY

CONTENTS

◀ Concarneau, *page 51*   ▲ Auray, *page 88*

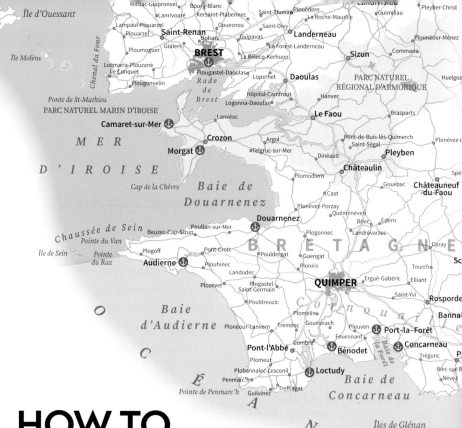

HOW TO USE THIS BOOK

This book starts in the city of Brest at the far western end of the massive 33,670 sq km (13,000 sq mile) Brittany peninsula that bravely sticks its nose far into the Atlantic Ocean. Taken as a whole, Brittany has 2,735km (1,700 miles) of coastline. Here, we follow that part from Brest as far south and east as La Rochelle on the Biscay coast, which tends to be as far as most UK sailors venture, the remainder of the coastline as far as the Spanish border being less attractive to many.

The south coast of Brittany is quite unlike the north coast, the English Channel-facing coast. Although the south side of the peninsula is open to the Atlantic and the often bad-tempered Bay of Biscay, in the summer months the weather is reliable, calmer and noticeably warmer than in the north. The sea is bluer as well. As you

make your way further east and south, the climate warms even more, the towns and villages start to develop a Mediterranean feel, and you begin to feel far from home.

Where north Brittany can present a craggy, rock-strewn face, the south is famous of its lengthy, clean, sandy beaches and sand dunes – someone counted 60 beaches in south Brittany.

The south coast is split into the administrative departments of Finistère, Morbihan and Pays de la Loire, which includes the Loire-Atlantique. Breton traditionalists will argue whether Loire-Atlantique is part of 'old' Brittany or not, and it's not a simple question and views are strong, so is best avoided. What's clear is that this book covers

that area that is known to all sailors as 'south Brittany'. I'll leave others to argue over where the actual lines are drawn.

A strange feeling can come over you at the end of a passage, especially to somewhere unfamiliar and outside your own country. You've been focused on your navigation, the tides, the landmarks; you have concentrated so hard on finding your way into a marina

▲ South Brittany – for blue, warm water and sandy beaches. What more could you ask for?

and getting into an unfamiliar berth that you've hardly had a moment to think about what happens next. That is when this book becomes your new friend.

Be clear – this is *not* a book to be used for navigation, although I do offer you anecdotal descriptions of what's broadly required to make it safely into harbour, no more than that. But when it comes to finding your way around once you are ashore, that is when this book comes into its own. When the boat is secure and the paperwork is done, close all those pilot books, fold away the charts or switch them off, and turn your attention instead to what lies in store as you head for the shore.

I've tried to give a flavour of the safest and most secure harbours along this wonderful stretch of French coastline. Of course, there are plenty of anchorages in which you might want to linger, but I have assumed that you will not be happy spending lengthy periods ashore unless you can be confident of the safety of your boat. That's why all the harbours in this book are those with marinas that offer complete security, where you can lock up the boat and walk away from it with peace of mind.

I know from experience that it is frustratingly easy to visit a town, only to discover after you've left it that you missed its best attractions. I've tried to point you in the right directions and offer you a sense of the often-rich history of these places. For cyclists, I've suggested the nearest cycle hire shops, and for walkers I've given an idea of walking times from the marina office.

When you've got children on board, there's an extra pressure to provide entertainment and I've tried to highlight some of the opportunities, even if it's only a beach – and there are some fabulous ones along this coastline. For shops, I've offered you only the nearest, knowing that an urgent need for teabags has to be met with haste. That shop might not be the largest, cheapest or best, but it's handy and that is often what matters most.

Having said all that, I suppose this is a navigation book of sorts, but one for which you don't need to climb into oilskins and harness. So, put on your walking shoes instead and enjoy the shores of south Brittany.

▼ This is the land of large, safe marinas – ideal places to leave a boat and explore ashore

SAILING TO FRANCE – AND COMING BACK

Following the UK's departure from the EU, and the complexities of Covid-19, it's not as simple as it once was to sail to France, although you can make it less painful with a bit of forethought and planning.

Be aware that procedures are being developed and changes introduced. French harbours and marinas are helpful in pointing you in the right direction and their website might offer advice.

When leaving the UK, or returning, you need to inform the UK's Border Force. This used to be done by filling form C1331 and returning it by post, which you can still do.

The online system is much more convenient and is designed to be easily accessed via a phone or tablet, at spcr. homeoffice.gov.uk/. Here you can open an account for repeated use, add crew names and details and update your cruising plans.

At the time of writing (2022), an online form can also be downloaded from some French harbour/marina websites. You are required to enter France by an official port of entry where passports, etc can be stamped and customs conducted, although this is expected to be widened to other harbours. It is important that you get stamped both in and out of France, as your stay in Europe is now time limited. If you fail to check out, they will assume you are still there and won't let you in on the next visit.

This may entail some time spent trying to find various offices to complete the formalities and you should build this time into the

schedule. This might seems onerous but it is early days and we can expect some streamlining, hopefully in place from the 2023 season onwards.

Don't rely on anecdote culled from websites – harbour/marina offices and websites are the best sources of information.

For the moment, the best advice seems to be:

● Have a Q flag on board to show when you arrive in France, and again when you return to the UK.
● Hold passports with at least six months left on them before they expiry.
● Carry your boat registration certificate (and VAT documents, see below).
● You may need proof of vaccination if there are any Covid-19 restrictions in place.
● Proof of boat's insurance and personal accident/health insurance, as well as a GHIC card, which replaces the old EHIC, and is available via the NHS website.

▲ It might seem like a bit of an effort to sail to France these days, but look at the coastline that awaits you

● Check the flares, liferafts, etc are in date.
● I would also ensure that I have the necessary devices to enable me to complete online forms, wherever I might be.

If you want to stay in France for longer than three months then you must apply for a Long Stay Visa, which falls outside the scope of this book. Likewise, the VAT regulations, which can become exceedingly complex depending on where you want to keep your boat if outside the UK, when you bought it, and where it might have been built in the first place. Again, it is better to take expert and informed advice on this rather than relying on anecdotal sources, of which there are many. Few of them are reliable.

FINISTÈRE

BREST ▶ BÉNODET

THIS PART OF FAR western France provides most people's introduction to the glories of south Brittany. It is roughly a 24 hr passage from Falmouth to L'Aber Wrac'h, where a break can be taken, and from there, by taking the tide, a day's sail to Brest, where South Brittany begins.

Finistère has managed to retain its feeling of remoteness, which, I should warn you, may be lacking in some of the harbours that lie ahead. While Brest is its largest city, it remains a largely agricultural part of France where Breton survives as a language

▲ Soak up the stunning landscape in Presqu'île de Crozon

along with Breton music, which reveals its Celtic influences.

From a sailing point of view, Finistère demands some effort before sharing its delights. You will have to pass through the Chenal du Four with its navigational stresses and speedy tides, and then face the notorious Pointe du Raz, which can be overwhelming in bad weather, but a pussy cat if you time it right and choose your weather. Only then can you start to point your bows to the SE.

You may want to take in Camaret-sur-Mer to replenish stores or get your taste buds in tune with the Breton crêpes and *galettes*. Douarnanez overflows with maritime tradition, Bénodet offers shelter in its river, and the Glénan islands are a joy to sail through on a clear and sunny day.

The rocks of northern Brittany will soon be replaced by sand dunes and endless beaches; there will be swimming and paddling in clear water that is few degrees warmer than it is further north.

As you arrive in Finistère from the UK, you can honestly say you have turned a corner.

BREST

POINTE DU RAZ 20NM, BÉNODET 60NM, L'ABER WRAC'H 30NM,
CAMARET-SUR-MER 10NM

This is a major French city with two excellent marinas and as many marine support services as you could wish for. The Second World War flattened the place and the rebuilding on a grid system has led to a rather dreary city, certainly devoid of any Breton atmosphere – you will have to look hard to find any evidence of this place's traditional roots, although a few very old houses remain. It is nevertheless a first-class place in which to stock up and change crews, with many attractive anchorages in the Rade de Brest if weather prevents you from going to sea.

NAVIGATION

You can reach Brest at any state of tide and in any weather and, being a major French naval port, the buoyage is first class.

There are two marinas: the first on approach is Marina du Château; the second the Moulin Blanc marina. Both are of a high standard and have all facilities.

OVERVIEW

Given its hugely important strategic position, Brest could hardly be anything other than a major naval base, and it has been since 1631 on the instructions of Cardinal de Richelieu. In the Second

▼ Le Phare du Petit Minou welcomes you to the wonderful cruising ground in the la rade de Brest

▲ The city of Brest, much has been rebuilt since the Second World War

▶ Good views of the harbour from the Dajot public garden behind the commercial harbour

World War, it was an important landing place for US troops, but in 1940 it fell to the Germans, who used it to great advantage as a base from which to attack north Atlantic convoys bringing much-needed supplies to Europe. The Germans built massive concrete submarine pens that no amount of bombing was able to destroy. So severe was the Allied bombing that the entire city was destroyed. The Germans paid huge sums to help fund the rebuilding, which was done in the 1950s in a somewhat utilitarian style employing much concrete. Brest is now a major base for France's nuclear submarines and one of the world's major ship repair centres.

MARINA DU CHÂTEAU

Enter the marina, being careful to avoid straying into the nearby naval dockyard. This is a large marina so expect plenty of lengthy walking. The hinterland has an industrial feel to it. There are 100 visitor berths.

FOOD AND DRINK
● The nearest supermarket is La Cambuse (convenience store), 36 Quai de la Douane (10 min walk).

MARINA MOULIN BLANC

▲ Marina Moulin Blanc – just a hop, skip and jump away from the dual carriageway

● Monoprix (supermarket), 49 rue de Siam (20 min walk) with **Carrefour City** close by, at 41 rue de Siam.

The essentials:

FUEL Conveniently situated on the end of the pontoon directly ahead as you enter.

REPAIRS Travelift and all engineering and repairs needs are catered for.

FACILITIES Toilets and showers are on the marina – check in at the imposing modern harbour office on NW side of the marina.

LAUNDRY On the marina.

POOL Piscine de Recouvrance, rue de Maissin (30 min walk). A modern Olympic indoor pool with fitness area, spa and sauna. Afternoon and evening opening only. Piscine Foch, 25 ave. Foch (30 min walk). A 25m (27-yard) pool with a second smaller pool that's open Sunday to Thursday.

(Note: this marina is some distance out of town – number 3 bus takes 20 min to the city centre.)

Pay attention to the buoyage in the dredged approach channel. Turn to port on entering to find the visitor pontoon parallel to the harbour walls.

This marina is on the W side of the Anse du Moulin Blanc, which has a beach at its head but is close by a dual carriageway.

FOOD AND DRINK
● The nearest supermarket is **Intermarché SUPER**, 118 rue de Quimper (30 min walk, uphill from the marina), but delivery can be arranged.
● The capitainerie can provide supermarket transport but only to an inner-city supermarket smaller than the Intermarché above.

THINGS TO SEE AND DO
(Note: distances are taken from Marina du Château.)

Oceánopolis, Port de Plaisance du Moulin Blanc (15 min by taxi). This is a futuristic aquarium on a grand scale, and next to the Marina Moulin Blanc. There are 77 aquariums, 4 million litres (879,900 gallons) of seawater and 10,000 sea creatures. Many eating opportunities. Plenty here for a family to pass a stormy day.

Château de Brest, blvd de la Marine (10 min walk). This castle represents

1,700 years of history and is the oldest monument to be found in Brest. It is still in use by the French Navy – which makes it the oldest castle in the world still in military use. It also houses the **National Maritime Museum**. Here, you will find much naval history, alongside models, sculptures and paintings. The audio guide is recommended, and children will find it an easy and engaging visit. Tours take a couple of hours. Afterwards, don't forget to walk the ramparts for the best views to be found in Brest.

Conservatoire Botanique National de Brest, 52 Allée du Bot (15 min by taxi from Marina du Château, or 30 min walk from Marina Moulin Blanc). This was once a rubbish tip but is now a highly regarded botanical collection, open daily with free access. It curates threatened Breton species both in the

The essentials:

FUEL 24 hr with credit card or pay at the harbour office at the head of the visitor pontoon.

REPAIRS All kinds of repair are within easy reach of the marina.

Head for the rue Alain Colas, which runs alongside the marina entrance (5 min walk) and you will find a multitude of chandlers and yacht services. Enquire at the capitainerie who may recommend one best suited to your needs.

REPAIRS There's a chandlery.

FACILITIES First-class showers and toilets within the capitainerie at the head of the visitor pontoon.

LAUNDRY Located near the capitainerie, at the head of the visitor pontoon.

▼ The remarkable lighthouse on Pointe St-Mathieu – the gateway to southern Brittany

open air and under glass, and houses plants from China, America, Australia and New Zealand.

The Naval Base, route de la Corniche (20 min by taxi) is open to visitors (ID required). An essential stop for lovers of military history, the Battle of the Atlantic and German submarines. The bunkers will amaze you. Tours in French and English.

The Brest International Maritime Festival has grown into a legend among lovers of traditional sailing craft. Held every four years, it attracts 700,000 visitors to see 1,500 craft. The next is due in 2024.

Ushant: if your sailing plans don't include a visit to this attractive island at Brittany's westernmost point, a ferry service operates twice daily, run by Penn Ar Bed, who also provides a service from Brest to Molène, Le Conquet and Camaret-sur-Mer. Look for its distinctive blue-and-white livery. Penn Ar Bed is located in the Port de Commerce (10 min walk to the NW of the marina).

You can also fly to Ushant with Finist'Air from Brest Bretagne Airport (see below).

FOOD AND SHOPPING

- There is no shortage of markets in Brest with at least one every day; some are morning markets and others open in the evenings. If you go for a stroll, take a shopping bag - you never know where you might come across one.
- Start with Les Halles St Martin indoor/outdoor market, which is open every day except Sunday from 0700 at 4 rue Massillon (35 min walk).
- The Sunday market to be found at 70–64 rue de Siam (20 min walk) starts early and tends to close around midday.
- A Sunday market operates at Place St Louis (25 min walk) with food and crafts, Breton dishes, roast chickens and charcuterie.
- For a treat, look out for canelés, a sweet speciality consisting of a local pasty that's brown on the outside with a rum and vanilla-flavoured custard on the inside. Try La Toque Cuivrée, 29 rue de Gouesnou, for the best.
- Strawberries and cream might sound a little routine, but the best in France are grown in nearby Plougastel.
- Alternatively, try a Molène sausage, which is smoked in seaweed.

FURTHER AFIELD

TGV trains run from Brest towards Paris (3 hr 30 min) with connections to the ferry terminal at Roscoff for crew changes – change at Morlaix.

Brest Bretagne Airport (20 min by taxi to the NW of the city at Guipavas) is mainly a charter base, but scheduled flights are operated by Air France so there are good flights to Paris and within France. Some UK operators offer flights from the UK during the season. A shuttle bus (Bibus) operates from the city centre to the airport (20 min).

The SNCF station (tall clock tower and semicircular passenger area) is found at 8 Place du 19eme Régiment d'Infanterie (20 min walk).

Tourist information: Place de la Liberté, 8 ave. Clemenceau (25 min walk)
Web: www.brest-metropole-tourisme.fr
Tel: +33 2 98 44 24 96

CAMARET-SUR-MER

BREST 10NM, **L'ABER WRAC'H** 38NM, **POINTE DU RAZ** 20NM, **DOUARNANEZ** 24NM

This is one of the most popular of all French harbours for those arriving from the UK. With easy access, good shelter and a charming, compact town, it's an ideal place to catch the tide south to the Pointe du Raz, or northwards to the Chenal du Four.

NAVIGATION

There are two marinas to choose from. Port Vauban is the first as you come round the breakwater, with plenty of space for visitors. Further into the harbour, you find two more marinas, Port du Notic and Port Styvel. Styvel is for local boats only; Notic is the one to port coming in and is your second option after Port Vauban. There are white visitor moorings in the bay. If aiming for the inner harbour, pay careful attention to the buoyage – yellow buoys mark the shallow areas. The famous derelict fishing boats, hauled above the high water (HW) line, will keep watch on you.

OVERVIEW

Apart from its obvious maritime connections, Camaret-sur-Mer has been a regular haunt of writers, painters and poets so expect to stumble across art galleries as you wander the back streets. The Battle of Camaret in 1694 resulted in embarrassment for the English when an amphibious landing,

▽ The Camaret-sur-Mer seafront, quiet for a change

part of an attempt to seize Brest, went disastrously wrong.

In the 18th century, this was a major centre of the sardine fishery, but when they became overfished, Camaret-sur-Mer turned to lobster and became one of Europe's largest lobster ports. It seems they didn't learn their lesson for the lobster soon became overfished and so now they trawl for tourists quite successfully.

This was the birthplace of the submarine in 1801 when an American, Robert Fulton, tested the first ever underwater craft, the *Nautilus*, which leaked a lot and was driven by oars. His sights were set on doing damage to a British frigate, but while he was struggling beneath waves the frigate sailed away.

THINGS TO SEE AND DO
Without leaving the harbour, the old church and tower are worth a visit.

▲ The inner harbour at Camaret-sur-Mer

▼ Camaret-sur-Mer back streets, once the haunts of writers and artists

Both are clearly visible from either marina and 10 min walk away. The **Tour Vauban** was built in 1689 to defend the port of Brest. Visitor access has been much improved in recent years and it is now a World Heritage Site. There are tours, in English, guided by iPads that you are given on arrival.

The chapel close by is the **Chapel of Our Lady of Rocamadour** (10 min; it was

▼ The rotting hulks of Camaret-sur-Mer

built between 1610 and 1683, but there have been places of worship on this site since the 12th century. It was destroyed by fire in 1910 and what you see is a restoration. There is much maritime atmosphere to enjoy while spending a quiet moment here.

Just beyond the harbour wall is the Plage du Corréjou – a terrific beach.

The Camaret Loop is 17km (10.6 miles) of wonderful walking that takes you round the peninsula behind which Camaret-sur-Mer nestles – you need to be quite fit for this one. However, there are several other circuits, which are less demanding. Tourist information will help.

The GR 34 walking route, which circuits much of Brittany, passes through Camaret. There are some spectacular coastal walks that will take you to Pointe de Pen-Hir and beyond, passing the memorial to the Free French forces, and past the giant granite Cross of Lorraine, which was inaugurated by Charles de Gaulle in 1951. Get a good map and discover many beaches along the way.

The Battle of the Atlantic Memorial Museum (20 min) sits overlooking the ocean towards Pointe de Pen-Hir, a pleasant stroll from the harbour. The museum is housed in a German bunker built as part of the Atlantic Wall and is easily visible from a distance thanks to the remarkable collection of anchors that stand guard.

Brittany is famous for its megalithic monuments, and those near Camaret-sur-Mer are known as the 'Standing stones at the edge of the world'. The stones are on open land to the W of the town along the road to Pointe de Pen-Hir and consist of large, white quartz blocks set in three lines. There might be over a hundred stones in all. They may date from 3000 BCE.

◄ There's a strong maritime feel to this small church by the sea

FOOD AND SHOPPING

- U Express, rue des Sardiniers (12 min walk).

▲ For your first crêpe in Brittany?

▼ The Vauban tower, surrounded by beautiful waters

FURTHER AFIELD

The nearest rail station is in Brest, 8 Place du 19eme Régiment d'Infanterie (1 hr by taxi), with high-speed connection to Paris (4 hr 16 min). Change at Morlaix for Roscoff and the ferry to Plymouth.

Bus route 34 runs between Brest and Camaret-sur-Mer (1 hr 30 min). Bus route 37 runs between Quimper and Camaret-sur-Mer (2 hr 25 min).

Penn Ar Bed operates a seasonal ferry between Camaret-sur-Mer and Brest. Check at its office at Quai Louis Auguste Téphany (15 min walk towards the fishing harbour).

Tourist information: 1A rue des Quatre Vents, a modern glass box of a building (15 min walk on the far side of the harbour). The capitainerie will have basic information.
Web: www.crozon-tourisme.bzh
Tel: +33 2 98 27 93 60

MORGAT

▲ A compact resort with a splendid beach

▼ An off-the-beaten track kind of harbour tucked neatly away

DOUARNANEZ 12NM, **AUDIERNE** 28NM, **POINTE DU RAZ** 15NM, **BREST** 25NM

Lying on the S side of the Crozon peninsula, this place feels, for a sailor at least, as if it's off the beaten track. The village is packed in July and August with visitors drawn to its wide beaches (very safe bathing) and pine-clad shores. It's a resort, pure and simple, and laid-back. It's a good stopover for a couple of days and children will love it.

out for a green post off the end of the breakwater. A long, straight pontoon dead ahead is dedicated to visitors. You can anchor in the bay or use one of the white mooring buoys N of the marina.

OVERVIEW

Strictly speaking, Morgat is only that bit of the resort close to the marina; Crozon to the NE is the main town,

NAVIGATION

This is a safe and secure marina, well tucked in. If you're coming up from the SW, you might have an anxious time trying to spot it. Look out for a shoal patch N from the breakwater marked by a red can. Also look

▲ A safe and sheltered marina, close by the town and beach

but the two blend seamlessly. This was once a major sardine port until it discovered tourism in the late 19th century, hence the beachside mansions built by rich Parisians. The major development of the resort was inspired by the Peugeot brothers in the 1930s – they went on to a great career in car building so blame them for the clogged streets of Crozon.

The essentials:

FUEL On the visitor pontoon, where it joins the shore.

REPAIRS Lifting facilities on the hardstanding by mobile crane.

CHANDLERY Close by the U Express (see below). For repairs, it's best to head down to Douarnanez or N to Camaret-sur-Mer.

LAUNDRY On the marina.

HIRE Bike and kayak rental – Crapato Bicyclo, 4 Place D Ys (5 min walk), next to the tourist office on the blvd de la Plage.

FERRY There is a daily ferry service to Ushant in the season, subject to weather.

Have no fear of not locating good food here – almost every cuisine can be found a short walk from the harbour.

THINGS TO SEE AND DO

There is a small **beach** dedicated to swimming on the outside of the breakwater – cross the marina car park. Swim within the yellow buoys, where boats and watercraft are not allowed.

Good **walking** is to be had all around this coast. Take **swimming** kit as there are many secluded beaches to enjoy.

Grottes de Morgat is a series of stunning caves on the peninsula between Morgat and the Cap. It's probably too far for the dinghy, but boat trips can be found from Morgat to Cap de la Chèvre, Cove of the Virgin Island, Pointe de Pen-Hir. Gustave Flaubert bathed here and wrote: 'The day illuminates the caves strangely, breaking at the angles and illuminating with a greenish light the damp walls where the softest tints blend together.' Contact Vedettes Sirènes, Quai Kador, on the marina.

▼ The Grand Hotel speaks of a time when this place was highly fashionable

▲ Bike hire is available right on the marina

▲ All personal watercraft are for hire, plus tuition

Centre Nautique de Crozon Morgat (on the marina). For families who want to widen their sailing skills there is kayaking, windsurfing, paddle boarding and dinghy sailing with all equipment available to hire.

Piscine Nautil'Ys, 1 rue Alain (25 min walk) is behind the beach opposite the substantial Grand Hotel. Top-class swimming pool with flumes.

The World's End Festival, 'Festival du Bout du Monde', is a live music festival with events scattered around the Crozon peninsula, usually held on the first weekend in August.

▶ The house that Eiffel built, with some rust to prove it

Villa Ker Ar Bruck, 2 rue Myrdhine (10 min) is a single-storey house designed by Gustave Eiffel of tower fame, built using iron sheets on an iron framework. This is a sparkling-white house, not as grim as its construction might suggest, located on the waterfront due N from the marina entrance.

FOOD AND SHOPPING
- The nearest supermarket is U Express, Allée des Tilleuls (10 min walk).
- From mid-June to September, there's a large **market on the beach** on the first and third Wednesday of every month (5 min walk from the marina).

- If you want to go into Crozon, there is a **farmers' market** every morning in the Place de l'Eglise (35 min walk).

FURTHER AFIELD
Train connections from Brest, 1 hr 30 min by bus (No. 34) from close by.

There is a twice-daily bus service to Paris for less than £20, but it takes almost 12 hr.

Tourist information: Place d'Ys (on the roundabout) (5 min walk)
Web: www.crozon-tourisme.bzh
Tel: +33 2 98 27 29 49

▼ Much eating and shopping is available on the Morgat waterfront

▶ (*Overleaf*) Almost a 'secret' coastline close to Morgat – expect rocks, caves and beaches

DOUARNENEZ

POINTE DU RAZ 20NM, **MORGAT** 10NM, **BREST** 30NM, **AUDIERNE** 30NM

If you cross from the Pointe du Raz directly to Camaret-sur-Mer or Brest, you are missing this treat of a harbour to be found at the E end of the Baie de Douarnenez. The town itself in on the E bank of the river with areas of narrow streets, fishermen's cottages and traditional crafts. The marina to starboard is at Tréboul. There is a strong maritime flavour to this place. Expect to see lots of tan sails and good beaches. And if you like sardines, so much the better.

NAVIGATION

The town is easy to identify and the river is easy to enter. The commercial and fishing harbours to the E are closed to yachts. On entering the river, you will see a long visitor pontoon on the W side, followed by the marina at Tréboul with visitor berthing on the first pontoons you come across, although these may be reserved for long stays. There is also a marina at Port Rhu on the E bank beyond a road bridge but with tidal restrictions due to a lock that holds back water to create a deep area for the exhibits at the maritime museum.

The visitor berths are often full, with rafting up, and are somewhat exposed. In poor weather, Port Rhu is the better option.

▼ The quieter harbour at Rosmeur – no yachts but there's an anchorage outside the harbour

▲ The marina at Tréboul is an attractive place

▶ Traditional and modern craft above the lock on the E bank of the river

OVERVIEW

The best years for Douarnenez were in the 19th century when this part of Brittany enjoyed the sardine fishing boom. It was recorded that in 1924 the fleet brought in one hundred million sardines over a six-month period. For a sense of tradition, look for the Quartier du Vieux Port. Unusually, this was a centre of communism in the first half of the 20th century due to problems faced by the sardine factory workers. The town had a communist council from 1921 to 1940 and was nicknamed the 'red town'. Although fish canning still takes place here, it has largely been rebranded as a living museum.

▼ A great place to sit and watch boats old and new

The essentials:

(Note: all distances are from Marina Tréboul.)

FUEL The fuel berth at Tréboul marina is found just inside the main part of the marina on the right.

REPAIRS A chandlery can be found at the S end of the main marina, offering electronics, shipwrights and engine repairs.

AMENITIES The marina office at Tréboul is found by walking from the visitor pontoon towards the main marina.

FACILITIES The toilets here are unisex.

LAUNDRY On the marina, but there are also open-air machines in the supermarket car park at 12 rue Etienne Kernours, but a long way out of town (8 min by taxi).

▼ Plenty of glimpses of old Douarnenez are possible in the older parts of town

THINGS TO SEE AND DO

The **Port Museum** has taken over the whole of Port Rhu and the waterfront where you might find, among others, a Norwegian coaster, steam tug, sardine rowboat and an Arab dhow. And, for some reason, the old Scarweather lightship.

Ashore, there are **art and photography exhibitions** as well as fine **maritime collections**. You can easily immerse yourself for a whole day in here, and probably come back the next day for more

Chapel of St Helen, rue Anatole France (30 min walk), is dedicated to the mother of Roman Emperor Constantine. What you see is a rebuild of 1755 using much of the original stone. The multicoloured wooden statue of St Helen is from the 1600s

and was built by Navy shipwrights.

You will have passed Île **Tristan** on your port side as you entered the river. There was once a priory here, but its claim to fame is that the sardine industry started here when the first canning factory was built. It is now a **Marine Park**, which you can walk to at low water (LW), the window for crossing being about 2 hr. The precise times are shown where the path meets the mainland. The **tropical gardens and orchards** are still maintained.

The **Maritime Festival** is unmissable for lovers of traditional craft. On offer is music, street food and more craft together in one place than you can imagine. The atmosphere is truly magical. It happens every two years. If it coincides with the Brest Maritime Festival, it can feel as if every traditional boat in the world has come to Brittany for the summer.

FOOD AND SHOPPING

● The nearest convenience store, **Marché de Tréboul**, 11 Quai de l'Yser, is a 5 min walk passing the

Boulangerie de l'Yser on the way, at number 21.

● The are many inviting boulangeries, charcuteries, cafés and restaurants as you walk onwards from the capitainerie.

● If you need a hypermarket, use E. Leclerc Douarnenez, rue de Toubalan (20 min walk).

● There is a market on Wednesday and Saturday mornings in Tréboul, on the marina car park, past the capitainerie.

● In Douarnenez, there is a fresh food and seafood market every morning in Place des Halles (30 min walk), except on Sunday. This is a traditional meeting place, a centre of the town's life.

● Look out for *kouign-amann*, which is a cake largely made of sugar and butter that has become almost an emblem of the town. It is flaky bread, light and caramelised on the outside. Like many traditional dishes, it was the creation of a local baker, Yves-René Scordia, who in 1860 ran out of cakes and so threw together what came to hand. His cake is now a legend. Try it at Maison du Kouign Amann, 5 rue Jaurès (30 min walk).

● Although yachts are not allowed in Port du Rosmeur (20 min walk), the waterfront has a less developed feel with many cafés and shops, fish for sale and fishing expeditions.

FURTHER AFIELD

Buses to and from Douarnenez stop outside the tourist office. Buses to Quimper (trains to Paris), Pointe du Raz, Audierne and Locronan.

The nearest airport is at Lorient, 45 min from Quimper by train, 35 min by bus to Quimper.

Tourist information: 1 rue du Dr Mével (25 min walk), just up from the museum
Web: www.douarnenez-tourisme.com
Tel: +33 2 98 92 13 35

▼ The museum begins above the lock, with the town to the left

▲ Ship restoration occurs in all parts of the harbour/museum

AUDIERNE

LE GUILVINEC 20NM, BÉNODET 30NM, POINTE DU RAZ 10NM

This is a fishing village turned attractive resort with plenty of Breton atmosphere and lots of summer visitors. It sits on a bend on the Goyen River, pretty much hidden from view if you are approaching from sea.

NAVIGATION

A useful place since it is the only decent harbour on this stretch of coast with a good anchorage close by at St Evette if waiting to make passage through the Raz. It's a tight little spot so don't stray too far from the marked channel and leading lines, but it's worth the effort. The approach is narrow and shallow in parts so the tides need to be worked and are safest 3 hr +/- HW. There is room for visitors in the marina, but be aware that some berths have a speedy tide running through them. It was created out of the original fishing harbour and retains a workmanlike atmosphere. The harbour master is friendly and helpful.

OVERVIEW

Prawns and crayfish were once a speciality here, but only a few oyster beds are left of what was once a thriving fishing industry that did big business with England and Belgium in particular. From a time around 1900, the lace industry replaced fishing. Much of the old architecture has survived and there are plenty of 17th- and 18th-century buildings along the waterfront. Enjoy the pathway known as the 'chemin de halage', which crosses

▼ A snug marina, but watch the fast flow of the tide

▼ A decent waterfront with bars and cafés the full length

the harbour and seems at its busiest with evening strollers. Close by is the fine, sandy beach to the S of the town, Plage des Capucins (15 min walk) with crêperies on the way.

◀ A memory of Audierne's traditional fishery

The essentials:

FUEL A recently installed fuel berth means fuel is now available both at Audierne and St Evette – credit card needed.

REPAIRS This is not the best place for any serious repairs but ask at the harbour office as engineers may be available.

CHANDLERY Some chandlery, clothing, surfboards etc at Comptoir de la Mer, 17 Quai de Jean Jaurès (3 min walk) to the S of the marina.

FACILITIES Toilets and showers on the marina – cross the road to find the harbour office with flags outside. It's the white building towards the N end of the marina.

LAUNDRY On the marina, but also try Laverie Du Port, 2 Place de la République (5 min walk).

▼ The beach, just S of the marina

THINGS TO SEE AND DO

A day trip to Île de Sein. If you don't fancy the navigation, an easy way to see this windswept rocky island is to take the ferry from the quay at St Evette (40 min walk). Ferries are operated by Penn Ar Bed or Finist' Mer (summer only). Takes 1 hr.

St Evette itself is worth a visit if you a seeking a quiet time, especially if you are anchored off there and waiting for the tide to head N. The beach is especially popular, plus there's a modest café on the shore and a dive centre on the quay.

L'Aquashow, rue du Goyen (7 min walk), close to the chandlery. All of Brittany's sealife is on display here – 1,500 species in giant tanks, touch pools for children. Bird life, too. Perfect family day out on a non-sailing day.

▲ There's lots of traditional Breton architecture in evidence here

Cap Sizun watersport centre, on the St Evette beach, and is a great place to try windsurfing, sailing catamarans and dinghies. There are qualified instructors and all ages are welcome. Noted for its friendliness.

FOOD AND SHOPPING

- There are any number of shops and cafés along the waterfront; bakery, butchers, pharmacy, coffee.
- For gourmet groceries, try Nourry Christine, 2 Place de la Liberté (5 min walk).
- For seafood, head to La Cotriade, 3 Quai Jean Jaurès (5 min walk).
- For stocking up, take a taxi to E. Leclerc Drive Audierne, route de la Pointe du Raz (5 min by car), passing Lidl along the way.

- The farmers' market on Saturday mornings on the harbourside is described as 'one of the prettiest markets in Brittany'.

FURTHER AFIELD

Buses to Quimper, then TGV connection to Paris (4 hr 30 min) and all parts of Brittany.

Tourist information: 8 rue Victor Hugo (3 min walk) – period building on the waterfront
Web: www.capsizuntourisme.fr
Tel: +33 809 10 29 10

▼ The green waters of Finistère surround Île de Sein

LOCTUDY

▶ White sands and blue waters of Loctudy

BÉNODET 5NM, **AUDIERNE** 27NM, **ÎLE DE GLENAN** 11NM, **LORIENT** 35NM

Laid-back and uncommercial, Loctudy is set in an attractive estuary with a traditional Breton village, Île Tudy, on the opposite bank. Good beaches are close by. It's a nice blend of busy fishing harbour and seaside resort.

NAVIGATION
Strong cross tides run through the visitor pontoons and there are generally fast flows in the estuary. No sailing in the approach channel 1630–1830 when the busy fishing fleet returns.

Little space for anchoring but some white visitor moorings NE of the marina. Watch out for the drying patch hereabouts. Call ahead and the marina staff will guide you to a berth.

OVERVIEW
This is a langoustine port that has thrived due to its safe and sheltered position with its back to the prevailing westerly winds, first recognised by

▼ Île Tudy, a miniature village across the water

▶ A narrow entrance. No sailing when the fleet is coming home

the monks who came here in the 11th century and founded the place. Apart from the sea, the surrounding land contributed to the prosperity, being first-class soil for growing vegetables and, in particular, potatoes. It is now a seaside resort, popular with those who like a quieter time.

THINGS TO SEE AND DO

Cercle Nautique de Loctudy, 14 blvd de la Mer (30 min walk to Plage de Langoz) This watersports centre, founded in 1937, organises training and holds regattas. Kayaks, dinghies, paddle boards and windsurfers are available for hire and instruction is given.

The essentials:

FUEL On the first pontoon/ concrete wave break you come to.

REPAIRS Volvo service centre in the fishing area, also chandlery. Coopérative Maritime on the marina – fashion, cosmetics and shackles. Pichavant Yachting, also on the marina, has a wide range of boatyard services and can arrange sail repairs.

LAUNDRY Available on the marina (or see below at Carrefour).

HIRE Cycle hire from the harbour office but limited to 1 hr – used mainly for getting into town.

Aquatiko (on the marina) offers wet cycle rental, RIBs and jetski excursions under the eye of qualified instructors. Treasure hunts and organised games are an alternative.

Although called an island, Île Tudy is a charming taste of Brittany that actually sits on a peninsula across the water from Loctudy. It's a small village, described as a village in miniature, with the water coming almost to the front door. There is a small marina and a lengthy beach on the E side of the peninsula. A small tourist office is at

A quiet and compact marina
– watch the flow of the tide

5 rue du Port. There's a ferry service from the harbour at Loctudy, as well as boats to the Glénan islands.

Église St Tudy, rue de Poulpeye (10 min walk) is a 12th-century church in the town centre, but much modified from the original, notably the bell tower and the adjoining chapel from the 18th century. There is a disagreement over who St Tudy was; it might have been Tudy of Landévennec, who was a 5th-century Breton saint after whom the village of St Tudy in Cornwall is named, or possibly St Tudwal – one of the seven founder saints of Brittany.

FOOD AND SHOPPING

● **Carrefour Market**, 45 rue du Général de Gaulle (20 min walk), features washing machines in the car park.
● **Viviers de Loctudy** – splendid fresh fish on the fishing harbour close to the marina.
● **Market** day is Tuesday in the square in front of the Mairie, Place des Anciens Combattants (10 min walk). Opens 1 July, 0900–1230.

▲ There's not much choice in Loctudy, which makes a change!

FURTHER AFIELD

Nearest trains from Quimper with TGV line to Paris (4 hr 30 min). Bus 56C Loctudy–Quimper (about 45 min) from the bus stop at the Mairie, Place des Anciens Combattants (10 min walk).

Tourist information: Place des Anciens Combattants (10 min walk) Web: www.destination-paysbig ouden.com Tel: +33 2 98 82 37 99

BÉNODET

CONCARNEAU 10NM, GLÉNAN ISLANDS 10NM,
POINTE DE PENMARC'H 18NM

Probably the most visited of all the south Brittany harbours by UK sailors. Set on the lower reaches of the lovely Odet River, it offers a choice of sailing both in the bay and the river. However, it is hugely busy in July and August. The town itself offers splendid beaches and has a certain style to it. The quieter town of St Marine is on the W side of the river, with far fewer crowds.

NAVIGATION

The tides in the bay as you approach are quite weak, but in the river they can run strongly. For a quiet life, try to time it for slack water. Beware of the fast cross stream, which can run through the visitor berths in both marinas – it can be near impossible to get off when it's running hard. There are visitor moorings on both sides of the river, but often rafting in high season.

▼ Pleasure for all on the beaches of Bénodet

▼ Safe in all weather, but watch the run of the tide

OVERVIEW

Unlike many harbours in Brittany, which can trace their roots back to the fishing trade, Bénodet (meaning the 'mouth of the Odet') seems to have leaned more towards tourism with a cinema, marinas, several beaches, spas and a casino – everything a resort could wish for. This area is known as the 'Breton Riviera' for good reason. Bénodet has trees and flowers, low houses with their backs to the sea, and a beach no less than 3km (1.9 miles) long.

For escape, St Marine across the river by ferry is the place. This is a

▼ Don't miss out on this lovely river and harbour

▲ A rich and relaxing little town

The essentials:

FUEL Good fuel berth, easiest at slack water, on the Bénodet side between the two marinas. Delivery can be slow – look for a button that speeds it up.

REPAIRS Repairs, chandlery and electronic services are all available. Head to Electro Marine for engine repairs, on the marina.

LAUNDRY The marina facilities are good and modern, including the laundry. Or try Wash'n Dry, 50 ave. de la Plage (20 min walk) on the Bénodet side. There's also laverie automatique on the St Marine side in Combrit (5 min walk).

HIRE Cycle hire: Cycletty, 5 ave. de la Mer (20 min walk). Route Surface, 14a Imp. Ménez Roz (on the marina) has paddle boards for hire.

former fishing village with a small church and almshouses for retired fishermen. It's a good place in which to take a deep breath if tourism gets too much for you. Needless to say, this is a first-class base for a family holiday, with all recreations provided.

THINGS TO SEE AND DO

The rocky fringes of the beaches are excellent for rock-pooling with children. Expect crabs and mussels. The water of the beaches is exceptionally clear and clean.

Biscuiterie François Garrec, route de Fouesnant (45 min walk, 10 min by taxi). Experience a 30 min guided tour of a top-notch maker of Breton cakes and biscuits.

Musée du bord de mer, 29 ave. de la Mer (15 min walk) is a small museum celebrating sea and the seaside. There's also modern art, and local and yachting history. Free entry.

Miss Aqua Planet, route du Letty (10 min by taxi) is an aquagym,

thalassotherapy centre and pool where there are swimming lessons for small children in a heated pool.

Vedettes de l'Odet, 2 ave. de l'Odet (7 min) offers cruises to the Glénan islands, gourmet trips along the Odet River and guided river tours. From the same location, is Le P'tit Bac, shuttles between Bénodet and St Marine. Leaves from the old harbour in Bénodet (S from the marina).

FOOD AND SHOPPING
● Carrefour Drive Bénodet is a large supermarket, Domaine de Penfoul Bihan (20 min walk).

● Marché supermarket, rue du Meneyer (20 min walk).

Near St Marine:
● L'Épicerie du Port, 21 rue du Ménez, Combrit (7 min walk).
● Good fish is available on both sides of the river.
● Market in Combrit on Wednesday; in Bénodet on Monday.
● Be sure to try the *palet Breton* ('Breton puck') – a biscuit that's rich in butter, and salted. Breton butter is special for two reasons. First, the milk from which the butter is made comes from cows that graze the luscious meadows that the climate encourages. Second, because in times past Brittany was exempt from salt taxes, salt was liberally used in butter preservation. Hence the salty biscuits.

◄ The bare necessities are well catered for

▲ There's plenty of beach space for everyone S of the marina

FURTHER AFIELD

Take a trip up the Odet to Quimper (nearest anchorage if taking your own boat is 1.6km/1 mile S of the town). There's a Gothic cathedral, an old town with half-timbered houses and the Breton County Museum. It's reckoned to be the cultural heart of Brittany. Bus 41 (FlixBus) takes 40 min.

Airport at Quimper, also at Lorient, 45 min by train from Quimper.

The nearest train station is at Quimper. Change at Rennes and take the Marne-la-Vallée – Chessy TGV for London. Also trains to Paris.

Tourist information: 29 ave. de la Mer (15 min walk)
Web: www.benodet.fr
Tel : +33 2 98 57 00 14

▼ Bénodet is one of the most frequented places in the whole of South Brittany

GLÉNAN ISLANDS

PORT-LA-FORÊT ► CONCARNEAU

THE GLÉNAN ISLANDS are rarely missed by yachts cruising this coast. They don't have a marina so fall somewhat outside the remit of this book. However, there are visitor moorings and anchorages that offer some safety depending on wind direction.

The beaches are white and sandy, the sea is clear and warm, and on fine days visitors will tell you that they could just as easily be on tropical islands. And there will be a lot of visitors.

There are nine main islands, and several smaller ones. To help preserve the landscape there is no camping

▼ Glénan, with an enduring sense of mystery – and not a marina in sight

allowed here, and there is only one holiday cottage! This means that most people who come here pour off the tripper boats that leave from Bénodet, Concarneau and Port-la-Forêt.

In high season, you will be lucky to find a mooring, and the anchorages might be busy. If you find yourself in one of the above harbours, a tripper boat out to the island may be the most relaxing way of getting to Glénan. Having said that, at the end of the day when all the trippers have left, to sit in the cockpit of your own boat amid these islands and watch the sun go down is one of the great experiences of this part of Brittany.

PORT-LA-FORÊT

BÉNODET 10NM, **CONCARNEAU** 5NM, **GLÉNAN ISLANDS** 11NM,
LORIENT 35NM

This was once a quiet little river, hardly disturbed, then along came a 1,000-plus-berth marina in 1972, making it the largest in south Brittany. There's still some atmosphere to be found, but not in the marina complex itself. Still, it's a very good place for repairs or overwintering, situated 1.6km (1 mile) from the nearest town of La Forêt-Fouesnant.

NAVIGATION

From seaward, follow the green and red buoys. The visitor berths are well marked, dead ahead on entering. The approach to the marina is dredged to 1.2m (3.9ft) but there is some silting. Unless you have a shallow draught, don't enter at LW. Waiting buoys are available.

OVERVIEW

You may well tire of this vast marina after a while, and for escape you should head for the small town of Fouesnant, about 1.6km (1 mile) to the N. This is a rich farming area, so expect high-quality local produce, in particular the cider, claimed to be 'the very best'. A 'festival of the apple trees' takes place in May.

Many of the most competitive sailors have trained here – Jean Le Cam,

▶ This was once a quiet little river, until the marina arrived

Samantha Davies, Michel Desjoyeaux, Olivier de Kersauson – which has given this place the title 'Valley of the Mad'.

Fouesnant was a haunt of Proust, and many other writers, painters and sculptors came here to enjoy the atmosphere created by the cider orchards rolling down to the sea.

THINGS TO SEE AND DO

The beach at **Kerleven** is 1km (0.6 miles) long and is flat, loved by paddle boarders.

There are no major attractions close by the marina, and those on the other bank are some way out of town. **Fouesnant**, however, is a pleasant enough village to stroll through and sip coffee in, although it's a bit of a hike (1 hr walk).

Centre Aquatique Les Balnéides, 51 Allée de Loc Hilaire (15 min by taxi) – a watersports centre with a slide, two pools and lots of floating fun.

Cidrerie Menez-Brug, 54 Hent Carbon (15 min by taxi). Not a lot to see, but free tastings and high-quality cider on sale in the heart of Breton apple country.

Miellerie de Fouesnant, 102 route de

The essentials:

FUEL Close by the visitor berth.

REPAIRS All repairs and service facilities are available on this large complex.

LAUNDRY Available on the marina.

HIRE Bike hire is available from the capitainerie.

FERRY Vedettes de l'Odet offers ferry services from the marina to Île de Glénan, Bénodet, Loctudy and Concarneau.

◀ At 1,000-plus berths, this is the largest marina in South Brittany

◀ To escape marina life, it's a 1.6km (1 mile) walk to the nearest small town

Fouesnant Bénodet (15 min by taxi) – a honey-lovers' dream come true.

Nautical Centre Kerleven, route de la cale sud Port-la-Forêt, just to the S of the marina (10 min walk) – sailing school with lessons for small children, said to be very family friendly. Optimist, windsurfer, kayak and paddle board rentals.

Well-regarded golf course, **Golf de Cornouaille**, route du Mesmeur (15 min walk) to the N of the marina. Join by simply filling out a form at reception.

FOOD AND SHOPPING
For major shopping, you will need a taxi.
● **Carrefour Express Fouesnant**,

20 Place de l'Eglise (50 min walk/12 min by taxi).
● **U Express**, 4 rue de Kerneveleck, and **Lidl** in Fouesnant.
● There is a **Sunday market in La Forêt-Fouesnant**, Place de la Baie (15 min walk), selling local produce, cakes, fresh fruit and veg.

FURTHER AFIELD
The bus No 41 takes 15 min to Quimper, and from there are rail connections to all of Brittany and Paris. The tourist office sells bus tickets.

Airport at Quimper (Cornouaille) (40 min by taxi) and Lorient (45 min by taxi).

Tourist information: Next to the capitainerie, or in Fouesnant, 2 rue du Vieux Port (15 min walk) Web: www.foret-fouesnant-tourisme.com
Tel: +33 2 98 51 42 07

▲ The Sunday market in the nearby village is a must

▲ Traditional *far Breton*, a set custard-style pudding – delicious!

CONCARNEAU

POINTE DU RAZ 50NM, **LOCTUDY** 12NM, **BÉNODET** 10NM, **ÎLE DE GROIX** 27NM

It's a town of two distinct halves. There's a modern, bustling place that comprises most of what is known as modern Concarneau, deriving a lot of its wealth from fishing, which is a big industry here. But atop a long island in the middle of the harbour is the old town, connected to the mainland by a bridge. The island divides the yachts on the S side of the island from the fishing fleet to the N.

NAVIGATION

It's a low coastline and attention to the buoyage and beacons is needed. There is a considerable fetch from the SW from which the marina has little protection – winter storms have done considerable damage. Otherwise, it's easy at all states of tide and in most weathers. The visitor pontoon is 'D',

▼ Concarneau marina is not too big and is close to the town

▲ The sundial stands guard over the entrance to the old town

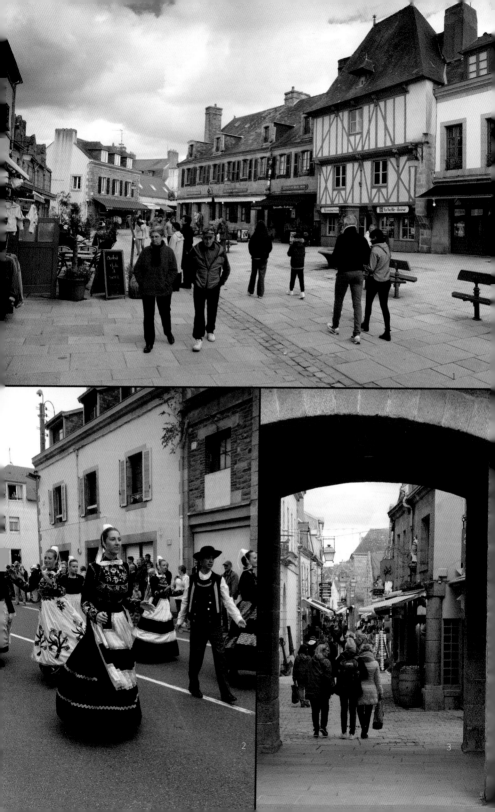

2

3

second from the N. You can also use the breakwater pontoon. You may not be able to find a space anywhere from mid-July to August.

OVERVIEW

Tuna fishing is big business here – 100,000 tons a year are landed – and the town has one of the last traditional tuna-canning factories. Tourism is healthy, many being drawn to the nearby sandy beaches, as well as boatbuilding, but remember that this is the third biggest fishing port in France. Traditionally, the Concarneau fishermen employed blue nets and their annual festival, Festival of the Blue Nets, held in August attracts thousands with a fishing interest, many wearing Breton costumes.

Most visitors, however, come for the 'Ville Close' 15th-century walled town, which looks down on the marina (see below).

THINGS TO SEE AND DO

Ville Close is the 15th-century walled town close by the marina, packed with shops and eateries that were once houses. Crowded in the season. Until 1373, this was English-held until they were chased away. Since then, it has been the scene of much military drama.

Musée de la Pêche, 3 rue Vauban (7 min walk) in the old town. Very fishy, a touch old-fashioned, but well done with guided tours giving a taste of this town's strong fishing connections.

◄ (Above right) There's always somewhere to leave the crowds behind and take a breath

◄ 1 Shop, bars and lots of atmosphere are to be had in the old town; 2 The festival of the Blue Nets; 3 I bet the old town on the island will be the first place you head for

The essentials:

FUEL Remarkably inconvenient fuel berth S of the marina. No floating pontoon – the pumps are on the shore. Not easy unless there are two of you.

REPAIRS For major repairs, seek advice from the harbour office; there is a wide range of engineering skills around the harbour complex.

CHANDLERY For chandlery/clothing/fishing gear, try Coopérative Maritime Concarneau, 4 rue des Chalutiers (20 min walk). Cornouaille Gréement, rue des Bolincheurs (30 min walk) for all marine services, including sailmaker.

FACILITIES The toilets and showers are accessed through the marina office, but only one toilet is open when the office is closed – someone didn't understand ease-of-use when they built this marina. To make it worse, the showers are reported to be quite small.

LAUNDRY On the marina, but restricted hours. Or, laverie automatique place de la mairie, Place de l'Hôtel de Ville (10 min walk).

HIRE Cycle hire: Hobby Cycles, 4 rue Henri Fabre (10 min by taxi).

▼ Historic walled-town of Concarneau

An old fishing trawler over which you can wander will give you a taste of life at sea as well.

Maison du Patrimoine de Concarneau, rue Vauban (7 min walk) – a 16th-century heritage house and home to the town's governor in the entrance to the old town – is a good place in which to get the atmosphere of the history of this place.

Marine Biological Station and Concarneau Marinarium, Quai de la Croix (5 min walk) is the oldest marine centre in the world. It was founded in 1859 and is still the home of a major research centre, employing 50 researchers. There is a complete aquarium and 120,000 litre (26,400 gallon) pool. At LW, it is possible to go down to the shoreline with guides to examine the richness of marine life.

Understand more about the Glénan islands and the current threats to all forms of marine life.

Beach walks are popular, and there is a pushchair-friendly route through Kérandon wood. The coastal path from Quai de la Croix takes you past impressive villas, ending up at the Sables Blancs beach.

FOOD AND SHOPPING

● The nearest supermarket is Carrefour City, 10 Place du Général de Gaulle (10 min walk).

● Expect to find no shortage of seafood for sale. Walk N from the marina towards the fishing harbour, then a couple of streets back you'll find the famous Les Halles covered market, Place Jean Jaurès (5 min walk), which, apart from fish, is good place for fresh fruit, veg, bread and Breton food, especially pancakes. Open 0800–1300.

- Also, **Poissonnerie La Roche Concarneau**, 5 Place Général de Gaulle (10 min walk) for more seafood.
- **Beer** is highly prized in Brittany, almost as much as their cider. Tri Martolod is the brewer in Concarneau. Brewing beer was started by monks who were seeking a less intoxicating drink. Since it was brewed from grains, it became known as 'liquid bread'. Having somewhat faded in recent years, the craft brewers and the micro-breweries are back. A good place to start might be **Hops! and Cheese**, 8 Place du Général de Gaulle (10 min walk) – a first-class combination of cheese shop and bar.
- There is a Monday and Friday **market** in the car park outside Les Halles covered market (see above) – fresh veg, meat, wine and takeaway food.

FURTHER AFIELD
There is an hourly bus service to Morlaix. Connect there for a bus to Roscoff for crew changes.

Trains from Concarneau station, avenue de la gare (20 min walk) – a very traditional and French-looking

station in the middle of the town – connects to Brest (approx. 2 hr 30 min) and Quimper (48 min), then onwards to all parts of Brittany.

Tourist information: Quai d'Aiguillon (10 min walk) overlooking the fishing harbour; very good English is spoken here
Web: www.deconcarneauapont aven.com
Tel: +33 2 98 97 01 44

▶ There's plenty of Breton atmosphere in the back streets

MORBIHAN
LORIENT
▶ ARZAL

(Including the Gulf of Morbihan)

▼ In settled weather you might
get to enjoy hidden beaches
like this one all to yourself

THIS REGION OF FRANCE gets its name from 'Morbihan', which means 'small sea' in the traditional Breton language that survives round here. Although this inland sea, the Golfe du Morbihan, is the obvious attraction of this region with its 30 or so islands (depending on how you count them), the variety of towns and harbours is huge.

It is home to the major centres of Lorient, Vannes and La Trinité-sur-Mer, but from a sailing point of view the rather more attractive and peaceful islands of Île de Groix, Belle-Île, Île Houat and Île Hoëdic offer excellent and often atmospheric harbours and anchorages. With the medieval town of La Roche-Bernard safely tucked away up the Vilaine River to the E, it would not be at all difficult to spend an entire cruise in the waters of the Morbihan district.

The sense of ancient history, first felt in Finistère, survives here. You will find ancient standing stones and other relics that are more common and older than Stonehenge. It is truly a land of legend, beaches and the best of Breton cuisine from galettes to cider, not forgetting the sauce 'Armoricain' (a rich sauce made from tomato, cognac and white wine) and endless feasts of mussels, lobster and Breton cheeses.

You are heading further south now and the water is getting warmer. No excuses for not taking a dip.

LORIENT

▶ The old submarine
bases at Lorient

ÎLE DE GROIX 10NM, BELLE-ÎLE 23NM, BÉNODET 35NM

This is Brittany's fourth largest city, rebuilt after the war, and a major commercial harbour with a choice of no fewer than five marinas. Like so many Breton cities flattened in the Second World War, the reconstruction has left it bereft of character. It's got a rather functional feel to it. Even so, it's a good place to take a break, in perfect shelter with every imaginable marine facility if you need repairs.

NAVIGATION
There is considerable shipping traffic – it's mandatory to keep watch on CH16 and keep out of the way. Cross-harbour ferry traffic needs attention. There is a well-marked approach, also with daymarks, and it is safe in any weather.

OVERVIEW
Prosperity came here in the mid-17th century when the French East India company was founded. Given its safety in all weather, it also developed into a major naval base and shipyard. The world's very first ship to employ a steel structure, the *Redoutable*, was built here.

In 1900, steam fishing vessels arrived and Lorient's importance as a fishing centre was established. It is now the second largest fishing harbour in France.

In 1941, the occupying Germans chose this as their submarine base, eventually building massive bomb-proof submarine pens that became the base for the U-boats employed in the Battle of the Atlantic. Some 4,000 tons of bomb were dropped by the Allies in an attempt to destroy the pens, but they failed. They bombed the city instead. Only a very few historical buildings remain standing.

They now call it the 'City of Five Ports' – military, fishing, passenger, sailing and commercial. Nearly half a million tourists a year leave this harbour on ferries bound for Île de Groix and Belle-Île. The navy has left, but the indestructible submarine pens remain and have been found a variety of uses, including bases for some of France's top racing sailors.

As mentioned, there are five marinas within the harbour area, all with different atmospheres.

◄ The imposing Port Louis Citadel marks the entrance to Lorient

WEST SIDE (STARTING FROM THE S)

Kernéval
A 30 min bus ride into town, but a short ferry journey (see below). This is a huge marina with 100 visitor berths, fuel and cycle hire available. It is close to the seaside resort of Larmor-Plage, which sprawls somewhat but has a pleasant, if small, town centre (30 min walk), which also brings you close to the splendid beaches.

This was once an important defensive area from which Lorient and the all-important East India Company was protected. It was from this town that Admiral Dönitz directed the Battle of the Atlantic.

FOOD AND SHOPPING
● Nearest shop: E. Leclerc Drive Larmor-Plage (large supermarket), Centre Commercial de Quelisoy (30 min walk).

Port de Plaisance de Lorient
If you want a city centre experience,

▼ The Fort de Porh-Puns marks the eastern side of the entrance to Lorient

this is the one to go for. Bars, cafés and shops line the quay. Good nightlife a short walk away. There are 50 visitor berths, fuel and all marine services.

FOOD AND SHOPPING
● Monoprix, 1 Quai des Indes (5 min walk).
● Supermarché Utile, 5 rue Adolphe Rondeaux (10 min walk).

EAST SIDE

Port-Louis
Located behind the Vauban citadel on the E side of the harbour entrance. There's a new capitainerie onshore that has improved the facilities in recent years. No repairs or maintenance facilities. It's not the best place if you have jobs that require assistance, but it's probably the cheapest of all the marinas, a quieter spot and close to an attractive town.

Locmiquélic
Recently upgraded shoreside toilet/ shower facilities, including laundry. No dedicated visitor berths, but they'll try to fit you in. No fuel here. The small town is only 800m (½ mile) away.

FOOD AND SHOPPING
● CocciMarket (convenience store), 2 ruelle de l'Église (10 min walk).
● Intermarché SUPER Riantec (hypermarket), Bellevue du loch (35 min walk).

Pen-Mané
This is the quietest option, situated at the mouth of the Blavet River. There are no shops close by but the waterbus to Lorient stops here (see below). This is a better bet than Locmiquélic is you are in need of repairs or services. (For shops, see Locmiquélic above.)

Cycle hire in town: use the self-service cycle hire scheme, Vélo An Oriant, 2 blvd Franchet d'Esperey.

THINGS TO SEE AND DO

(Note: no walking distances are given as distances to attractions vary wildly because of the widespread nature of the marinas around Lorient. Best to get a map from tourist information and plan from whichever marina you are in.)

Sous-Marin Flore, rue Roland Morillot. This tells the history of Lorient from a military and maritime point of view in an interactive museum. There are sound and light shows and you can walk into the *Flore-S645* submarine, which was launched in 1960 and once the flagship of the French Navy. 'Find the Spy' game (smartphone required). Designed to be enjoyed by all ages.

Keroman Submarine Base (Base des Sous-Marins), Presqu'île de Keroman. Tours of the U-boat base last about 1.5 hr. Discover how submarines work and how the crews live. See at first hand the sheer strength and resilience of these submarine pens. Films, archives and artefacts from wrecked ships.

La Tour Davis, part of Keroman Submarine Base (see above), was a training tank for French submariners, particularly underwater evacuations. It's a visit for committed submarine fans but has good multimedia and descriptions of the Battle of the Atlantic.

Cité de la Voile Eric Tabarly, Lorient La Base. You can spend a good half day here learning the ways of ocean-racing sailors and their specialised techniques. Model yachts, simulators, 3D cinema. And, of course, learn of the story of Éric Tabarly, one of France's greatest ever ocean sailors and designers. There's a reconstruction of the interior of *Pen Duick II* and lots of archive material. Great for all ages and

---

Harbour ferries

The easiest way to get around Lorient is to use the harbour ferries. These are operated by CTRL, which is the local public transport provider. There are five ferry routes and tickets can be bought onboard.

B1 Lorient Quai des Indes – Locmiquélic Pen-Mané

B2 Port-Louis La Pointe – Lorient fishing harbour

B3 Locmiquélic St Catherine – Lorient fishing port

B4 Gâvres pier – Port-Louis Locmalo

B5 Port-Louis La Pointe – Locmiquélic Pen-Mané

Summer-only routes:

B6 Lorient Quai de Indes – Gâvres pier

B7 Lorient Quai des Indes – Port-Louis La Pointe

---

designed for families to enjoy.

Musée de la Compagnie des Indes, Citadelle de Port-Louis. This museum, housed in the citadel close by the marina at Port-Louis, tells the story of the East India Company, one of the greatest of the 17th/18th-century trading companies. Learn how the French traded with Africa, Asia and America. There's Chinese porcelain, Indo-European furniture, ship models and recreations of intrepid voyages to the Orient.

Musée National de la Marine, Citadelle de Port-Louis. Also located in the citadel at Port-Louis, this comprises a collection of boats, historical models and maritime art – sea rescue is featured. The citadel itself is said to be one of the finest, with terrific views across the harbour and along the coastline.

Ferries leave from Lorient for Île de Groix (45 min journey).

The Festival Interceltique is held in August every year and is a major event including all Celtic nations, Cornwall, Wales, Scotland and Ireland among them. Expect Breton bagpipers, Irish fiddles and upwards of half a million people.

FOOD AND SHOPPING

● With the marinas so scattered, the best shopping advice will be available from the capitainerie. Lorient claims 17 supermarkets within the city.

● Markets – there are many – Tuesday at Halles de Merville, ave. Anatole France and Halles St Louis, 53b rue Jules le Grand; Wednesday at Place Aristide-Briand; Saturday at Halles Merville and St Louis (see above). (Markets seem to have a mind of their own and appear/disappear with speed. Best check first with tourist information before setting off on a major hike.)

FURTHER AFIELD

Lorient South Brittany Airport (15 min by taxi from Lorient centre) with regular flights to Lyon, Toulouse and Paris CDG. Flights to the UK in season.

Gare de Lorient, Place François Mitterrand (1km/0.6 miles N of the city centre) – trains to Quimper (35 min), Rennes (1 hr 30 min) and Paris by TGV (3 hr).

There are bus services from near the rail station to many French towns. Bus companies include Isilines, FlixBus and Ouibus.

> Tourist information: 45 bis blvd Cosmao Dumanoir – near the railway station (25 min walk from Port de Plaisance)
> Web: www.lorientbretagnesud tourisme.fr
> Tel : +33 2 97 84 78 00

▼ A misty dawn over Port Louis, Lorient

ÎLE DE GROIX

LORIENT 7NM, BELLE-ÎLE 21NM, CONCARNEAU 25NM

This is Brittany's second largest island, with 2,400 inhabitants and one harbour at Port Tudy on the N side. It's a granite lump just over 6.4km (4 miles) long but rich in geology not found on the mainland, ancient monuments, tall cliffs and many splendid sandy beaches. What's more, there are no less than 40km (25 miles) of cycle tracks and not a single traffic light on the island.

NAVIGATION
There are 50 visitor berths but expect them to be in high demand in the season. Entrance is straightforward except in strong NE wind – beware the

vent solaire (a NE land wind that blows in the early hours), which can blow quite strongly, even in settled weather. There is constant ferry traffic, which detracts from the peace of the place.

There are fore and aft moorings between white buoys in the outer harbour, pontoon berths in the inner harbour. Beyond that is a wet dock behind a lock gate.

OVERVIEW
Tuna was once king on this island, hence the hapless fish on top of the village church's bell tower. The big conundrum is why, in the area around Pointe des Chats, is the rare, bluish glaucophane found when the only other places in which it appears in the world are the Greek islands and in Greenland? If you believe in crystal therapy then you'll find it good for memory and sleep. It's an attractive island with small villages away from the main harbour and lots of excellent walking.

◄ Expect things to be cosy on Île de Groix

The essentials:

AMENITIES Water on the pontoons, and electricity.

FUEL None on the marina but in cans from the SE corner of the inner harbour.

REPAIRS Chandlery and some repairs are available on the harbour.

FACILITIES Showers on the quay S of the wet basin.

LAUNDRY On the quay S of the wet basin.

HIRE Cycle hire: Coconut's, distinctive building on the harbour. Bikini-Bike on the harbour. At the Green Bike, Le Gripp (6 min walk) W from the harbour. (Note: the coastal footpath is closed to bikes. If walking, the tourist office can provide maps and recommend good hiking behaviour given the nature sensitivity here.)

FERRY There are several ferries a day to Lorient, approx. 45 min.

▲ Good shopping with possible delivery to the harbour

THINGS TO SEE AND DO

The nearest beach to the harbour is **Côté d'Héno** (10 min walk). Look for the steps down to it.

Île de Groix has the only convex beach in Europe, **Les Grands Sables** (30 min walk, 10 min cycle), on the E edge of the island, shaped by sea currents and moving slowly to the W – 500m (550 yards) in the last 15 years. Fine white sand, clear water and lifeguards.

Locmaria beach (30 min walk) faces due S with shops nearby. Kayaks for rent. The village of Locmaria is itself worth pausing at as you pass through.

The **Red Sands beach** (45 min walk) is nicknamed the 'garnet island' – yet another of the region's geological peculiarities. This beach gets its name from when the sand has been stirred up by the sea and the garnet makes its presence felt. It is to be found at E end of the island.

◀ Lots of quirky buildings in the small town of Bourg

▲ Port Lay, with a good anchorage off in settled weather

Ecomusée d'Île de Groix, 49 rue du Général de Gaulle (10 min walk) is a museum focused on the history and heritage of social of the island. Close by the harbour.

The traditional house of Kerland (45 min walk). Bought by the town of Kerland, this is preserved as a glimpse of traditional life on the island. This small house was once the home of a family of six, and the exhibits ranging from everyday domestic utensils to farming machinery give a real insight into life here before tourism.

FOOD AND SHOPPING

● Carrefour Contact, Kermario (15 min walk), up the hill towards the village, with shops along the way.

● Contact Intermarket, route des Plages (15 min walk). It may be possible to arrange food deliveries to the harbour.

● Market day is in the main village, 800m (½ mile) walk from the harbour, on Tuesday and Saturday.

FURTHER AFIELD

The bus service operates on demand and does a circuit of the beaches, villages and hotels.

Tourist information: Close by the harbour above the ferry terminal (5 min walk)
Web: www.lorientbretagnesud tourisme.fr
Tel: +33 2 97 84 78 00

ÉTEL

MORBIHAN 30NM, **ÎLE DE GROIX** 10NM, **LORIENT** 9NM, **BELLE-ÎLE** 20NM

The entrance here is tricky, with a shifting channel that changes day by day. Don't even think about it unless conditions are perfect. It's worth the concentrated effort, though, as inside is a fine resort with a safe marina and a town with a thriving holiday atmosphere and one of the most charming of the Brittany rivers.

▲ Étel welcomes you, and points you to the berthing

NAVIGATION

The directions for entering are given from the shore either over VHF or from a semaphore station on the NW bank of the river. The movement of the semaphore arm will direct you to alter course as appropriate. *You must consult the pilot book in close detail* and have it close to hand. It's straightforward once you're inside and breathing again.

OVERVIEW

This was once one of France's major tuna ports and employed more than 1,000 people in the first half of the 20th century. Possibly more important these days is the oyster fishery, which produces 3,000 tons of oysters a year. On the S side of the entrance to the river are 8km (5 miles) of splendid sandy beaches fringed by endless sand dunes – a protected area. The town is compact and makes for pleasant strolling with many café opportunities close by the marina.

▼ It's more peaceful here than in other parts of Morbihan

▼ There are plenty of refreshment opportunities available on the quay

The essentials:

FUEL No fuel on the marina.

CHANDLERY Cooperative Maritime is on the quay S of the marina.

FACILITIES Shower and toilet block (modern building) by the capitainerie – halfway along the marina on the shore side.

LAUNDRY Blanchisserie de L'Ocean Le Blevec Nadine, 5 rue de la Libération (6 min walk).

▲ When you've managed to get this far, you can finally relax

THINGS TO SEE AND DO

Museé des Thoniers, 3 Impasse Jean Bart (5 min walk). This museum tells the story of tuna fishing from Étel's heyday when it was one of the most important fishing ports of France for both tuna and sardines. Much maritime heritage, an artist's view of the town and the fishing industry, and an emphasis on marine rescue.

If you are lucky enough to be here in August, expect to find the annual tuna festival where grilled tuna is served in large quantities on the quayside, with Breton sauces and good drink.

FOOD AND SHOPPING

● Carrefour Express, 7 blvd Charles de Gaulle (5–7 min walk). It's next to the cinema.

- **Market** day is Tuesday 0700–1300, Place de la République (8 min walk).

▲ A great place to stop and enjoy a crêpe!

▼ This is a town with a jolly feel to its shops and a cheerful atmosphere

FURTHER AFIELD
Bus No 16 runs between Étel and Lorient (1 hr). Bus No 18 runs Belz–Étel–Auray.

The nearest train station is at Auray, Place Raoul Dautry (30 min by taxi), TGV to Paris (2 hr 45 min).

Nearest airport is at Lorient (1 hr by taxi).

Tourist information:
1 Place des Thoniers
(2 min walk)
Web: www.baiede quiberon.bzh/etel
Tel: +33 2 44 84 56 56

BELLE-ÎLE

BÉNODET 50NM, **LORIENT** 25NM, **ST NAZAIRE** 40NM, **AURAY** 20NM

This is the largest island off the Brittany coast, and the gatekeeper to Quiberon Bay, which is at the centre of Brittany yachting. No one fails to be charmed by this place. There's only one harbour at Le Palais where you can lie alongside, but there is shelter at Sauzon and anchorages on both the north and south coast.

NAVIGATION

Be prepared for a tight little harbour. You can't miss the Citadelle Vauban on the N shore or the breakwater that runs to the S from it. There is much speedy tourist ferry traffic, so watch out. There are bow and stern moorings in the outer harbour, but a dinghy is needed. Beyond that, the inner harbour dries. To lie alongside, you must pass through lock gates (HW +/- 1 hr approx.) to the inner basin. Getting a berth anywhere is the summer can be a struggle – get in early. For peace and quiet, press on towards the marina at the very head of the harbour.

OVERVIEW

If you think the island is coming under assault from tourists, it's nothing compared to what it has suffered over the years. Pirates in the Middle Ages plundered here and foreign navies mounted assaults on it, hence the citadel at the harbour mouth.

▼ The waterfront at Sauzon, the main harbour on Belle Île

The essentials:

(Note: walking distances given from the wet dock entrance.)

AMENITIES The harbour office can be found on the landward shore of the outer harbour.

FUEL There is diesel and water at the inner end of the S pier (check the depth).

REPAIRS No facilities for major repairs, but Ilo Marine, La Saline (5 min walk at the far end of the marina), can offer maintenance, storage, chandlery and engine repairs.

CHANDLERY There is a Cooperative Maritime, ave Carnot (10 min walk).

FACILITIES Showers are close by the harbour office.

LAUNDRY Laverie AquaLogia, 34 ave. Carnot (10 min walk) or Laverie KISWash (in Super U et Drive, 15 min walk, S side of W basin).

HIRE Cycle hire: Au Cheval de Fer, 1 Bis Quai Gambetta (2 min walk) are electric bike specialists. Cyclélec, 3 Quai Bonnelle (7 min walk), close to the capitainerie. A Loca Scoot, 4 Quai Bonnelle (7 min walk), for cycles and scooters of all sizes.

FERRY There are ferry services to many Brittany harbours. The shortest crossing is to Quiberon (45 min); Vannes (2 hr).

▼ Clear inviting water for swimming at numerous bays around the island

There's a strong Welsh religious influence here; many villages are named after Celtic saints. Agriculture was once the mainstay, and shipbuilding at Le Palais, all gone now, of course, although some farms still thrive and the range of fresh produce to be bought here is mouth-watering.

There are 80km (50 miles) of footpaths to enjoy along both sides of the island, and 80km (50 miles) of cycle tracks. Among the reported 58 beaches (7km/4.3 miles of sand), you're sure to find a beach to suit you, and possibly a little peace and quiet on what can be a crowded island in the season.

In the deal of a lifetime, the British who occupied the island from 1761 agreed to give it back to the French in exchange for Menorca. Many of the

▶ 1 The picturesque inner harbour of Le Palais; 2 Popular restaurant for breakfast overlooking the harbour; 3 Detail from the Citadel walls; 4 The drying harbour at Sauzon; 5 Popular moorings outside Sauzon breakwater; 6 The dramatic Aiguilles de Port-Coton, as painted by Monet

1

2

GRAND HOTEL DE BRETAGNE

3

4

5

6

islanders can trace their ancestors back to Acadia, a French colony of north-east Canada, including Nova Scotia.

THINGS TO SEE AND DO
Musée Citadelle Vauban (10 min walk) covers a thousand years of history and provides some fantastic views over Le Palais with maritime museum of military and island history.

The island bus runs several times daily (from near the tourist office). There are two routes, one to the NW part of the island, the other to the SW. Purchase tickets on the bus.

Les Cars Bleus offers coach excursions from near the ferry landing stage.

FOOD AND SHOPPING
● Le Comptoir de Belle-Île en Mer, 2 ave. Carnot (7 min walk) is a high-quality grocers.

● SPAR, 38 rue Joseph le Brix (2 min walk) for less fancy needs.
● There is a daily market in the Place de la République (8 min walk). Late-night market on Tuesday and Friday in the summer.

FURTHER AFIELD
The nearest mainland train station is at Auray, Place Raoul Dautry. There are year round ferry services to Belle-Île from Quiberon (45 min), Vannes (2 hr), la Turballe (1 hr 50 min) operated by Compagnie Océane.

Tourist information: Quai Bonnelle (8 min walk)
Web: www.belle-ile.com
Tel : +33 2 97 31 81 93

▼ Sauzon – not much room here, and busy with ferry traffic

ÎLE HOUAT

Only 350 people live here and there are hardly any trees, and certainly no cars. It's a small island that manages to pack in rocks and moorland as well as lengthy beaches and clear, blue water. There are no step-ashore moorings.

NAVIGATION

Don't even think about trying to get into the tiny harbour, Port St Gildas (the adjoining village is called Houat). Moorings are outside in the bay. If the *vent solaire* is strong, you could have an uncomfortable night. Large ferries operate from here, so a sharp lookout is needed.

THINGS TO SEE AND DO

Cycling and walking is the best way to see the island, but a local bus service operates between the village, the

▲ Be ready to anchor off Houat – the harbour is tiny

harbour and the campsite. The island is only 4km (2.5 miles) long by 1km (0.6 miles) wide and walking the coastal path will provide you with the best of it – it takes about 4 hr to complete.

Eclosarium, route Ecloserie (on the SW side of the island) (15 min walk). This started as a hatchery producing lobster eggs but has developed into a major marine research centre. They describe the visitor experience as 'a voyage into a microscopic marine world'. Expect to get close up with plankton and understand more about the flora and fauna of the island.

FOOD AND SHOPPING

● It takes no longer than 5 min to walk into the town, where you will find a small selection of shops, and a **bar**,

---

The essentials:

AMENITIES It is safest not to expect any amenities: no fuel, no repairs.

For the harbour office, go to the Mairie (town hall).

FACILITIES There are showers up the hill that leads from the ferry berth. There are also showers on the E-facing beach on the end of island on a street called Le Bourg.

HIRE Cycle hire is available on the route du Port at the entrance to the village.

crêperie and at least three **restaurants** – book early.

- **Houat Market**, 197 route du Béniguet.
- **Boulangerie Ets le Gurun**, Le Bourg.
- **Perron Daniel-Votre Marché**, small convenience store, route du Vieux Port.
- **Propharmacie**, 134 Le Bourg (8 min walk), medical office.
- **Claudine Le Berre** (a gourmet grocery shop), route du Port.

▼ You will see plenty of interesting sights if you walk around ashore

▲ Port de St-Gildas is peaceful looking, but beware the busy ferries

FURTHER AFIELD

Ferries to and from Quiberon (45 min).

Tourist information: At the Mairie, Le Bourg (5 min walk)
Web: www.baiedequiberon.co.uk/houat
Tel: +33 2 97 30 66 42

ÎLE HOËDIC

ÎLE HOUAT 5NM, BELLE-ÎLE 12NM, PORT HALIGUEN 13NM, ST NAZAIRE 30NM

An island less than 1km (0.6 miles) wide and 2.5km (1.6 miles) long; low-lying with a rocky coast that breaks up the sandy beaches. No cars, and 100 permanent residents, rising to 3,000 in the summer, but you can generally escape them and find some peace and quiet. Most visitors say it has a relaxing atmosphere.

NAVIGATION

The harbour is called Port de l'Argol and is very small and busy with ferry traffic – don't try it. There is an anchorage

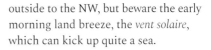

The essentials:

AMENITIES No fuel here, nor repairs or chandlery.

FACILITIES Water from the toilet block and showers on the harbour – look for the slipway.

outside to the NW, but beware the early morning land breeze, the *vent solaire*, which can kick up quite a sea.

▼ There are a few finger berths in Port de l'Argol and a few mooring buoys (be prepared to raft)

▲ A crowded island in summer, but always somewhere to escape to

THINGS TO SEE AND DO

Hoëdic Fort, S from the harbour on the far side of the village (15 min walk). A 19th-century fortification now used as a hotel and conference centre, but with public exhibitions by artists.

Nature rambles for all ages.

FOOD AND SHOPPING

● It is less than a 10 min walk to the small village, where you will find a **butcher, crêperie** and **restaurant.** You will be happier here if you arrive with a well-stocked boat.

● **Blanchet Serge,** Le Bourg (10 min walk) sells fruit and veg.

FURTHER AFIELD

Ferries to Quiberon and other harbours in the Morbihan, often via Île Houat (45 min journey time). At Houat, change ferries for Lorient operated by Compagnie Océane.

Tourist information: At the Mairie, Le Bourg (10 min walk)
Web: www.baiedequiberon.co.uk/ hoedic
Tel: +33 2 97 30 66 42

◀ No cars to worry about on this vehicle-free island

PORT HALIGUEN

BÉNODET 50NM, **VANNES** 20NM, **LE CROISIC** 27NM

You are now on the tourist trap they call the Quiberon peninsula and all that goes with it. It's a pleasant place with beaches and cafés but is somewhat lacking in atmosphere ashore. The town of Quiberon is a 30 min walk away. The peninsula is built up in many places, so don't expect to find too much open space close to the marina.

NAVIGATION

This a large, safe and secure marina giving total shelter from the W. There are no immediate dangers in the approach. The marina is divided, and in the past visitors were directed to the W part, but since extensive works the E part seems to be favoured. Because of the layout, expect some walking even to get to the shore. Bikes are popular in this marina with good reason.

OVERVIEW

This was once a small harbour protected by a simple dry-stone jetty until the coming of the marina in the 1970s. The fact that it has 11,000 visiting yachts a year speaks to its popularity – more modernisation is planned.

▼ A safe and secure marina, but expect some walking

▶ There's a lot of holiday home development around the marina

▲ Quiberon is a large yachting centre, so expect good facilities

Quiberon Bay itself was a popular spot for naval battles going back as far as the Romans. More recently, the Battle of Quiberon Bay in 1759 was one of Britain's greatest naval victories over the French, which, it is reckoned, greatly diminished the power of the French Navy for a generation.

Sardine canning was a big industry hereabouts, thanks to a scientist, Nicolas Appert, who developed a

The essentials:

FUEL You need the easternmost part of the marina. The fuel jetty is clearly seen at the head of one of the pontoons (24 hr with credit card).

REPAIRS Lifting and slipway on the marina. Marine Maintenance, 19 Bis rue d'Armorique (30 min walk, 6 min by taxi). Morbihan Nautical, 2 Port Haliguen, on the marina (10 min walk).

FACILITIES There are two toilet and shower blocks with laundries.

HIRE Cycle hire: Cyclomar, 47 Place Hoche (30 min walk). Cycles Loisirs SARL, 32 rue Victor Golvan (25 min walk).

FERRY Vedettes Angélus offers day-long Morbihan tours from the marina in July and August. There are ferries to Belle-Île (50 min journey) with Compagnie Océane, also to Houat (40 min journey) and Île Hoëdic (25 min journey).

▼ If you are wondering what the statue is staring at across the water…

▲ … it is his friend on the other pier

▼ Very good beaches are to be found just a short walk from the marina

technique for sterilising food that led to canning becoming a safe way of preserving food.

THINGS TO SEE AND DO

Centre équestre l'Eperon, 38 rue Jean Pierre Calloch (12 min by taxi), offers riding for all ages and skills.

Quiberon Aventure, blvd du Conguel, towards the tip of the peninsula (30 min walk). Adventure centre with zip wires and acrobatic courses. All ages and skills catered for, from four years upwards. Kids will love this.

Presqu'île Surf School, 28 route du Chemin de Fer (15 min by taxi). Suitable for everyone aged six and over, all levels of skill. Qualified instructors. Paddle-boarding lessons are an option, too.

Quiberon Plongeé, Port Haliguen II on the marina, offers diving lessons from the age of eight upwards. Beginners and families welcome. English is spoken.

▼ The nearest supermarket, Casino, is a short(ish) walk away

Golf de Quiberon, Chemin de la Trepetiniére (30 min walk). This is an 18-hole pitch and putt course, and a smaller nine-hole course. Instruction is available.

There are good beaches to the N of the marina – Plage de Castéro (15 min walk) and Plage du Porigo (10 min walk).

FOOD AND SHOPPING
There are limited groceries available on the marina, but for shopping, Quiberon is the place to head for:

• Casino Supermarché, rue de Port Haliguen (12 min walk towards Quiberon).
• Start exploring the many shops in the centre of town from Place Hoche (30 min walk).
• Market day in Haliguen is Wednesday, Place de Port Haliguen (10 min walk). In Quiberon, it's on Saturday on the Place du Varquez (30 min walk).

FURTHER AFIELD
There are buses to Auray (No 1, 1 hr) and Vannes, which stop at Port Haliguen.

SNCF station at Place de la Gare (20 min walk) offers a seasonal service only to Auray (50 min).

Tourist information: No tourist office in Haliguen (although the capitainerie may help). In Quiberon, 14 rue de Verdun (30 min walk)
Web: www.baiedequiberon.bzh/quiberon
Tel: +33 2 44 84 56 56

▼ A safe and weather-proof marina at Port Haliguen

LA TRINITÉ-SUR-MER

ÎLE HOËDIC 15NM, **PORT HALIGUEN** 8NM, **CROISIC** 27NM, **BELLE-ÎLE** 17NM

This is the home port of some of France's top-class racing sailors, which means there is no shortage of boatyard/chandlery infrastructure. If you've got a problem, this is the place to get it sorted. The waterfront is bustling, not to say overcrowded in season, and there are enough cafés/restaurants to keep you occupied for several weeks.

NAVIGATION

This is an oyster-growing area so mind the oyster beds. The channel is buoyed the length of the river, and the shelter in the marina is good largely due to a large mudflat, La Vanneresse, which gives it protection in southerly winds. However, it covers at HW and some swell can creep into the marina. The flow of the tide, and the river current, are felt in the marina. Pontoon D, first on the left, is for visitors. The capitainerie is at the head of this pontoon.

OVERVIEW

This was once a major harbour owing its prosperity to trade in cocoa, cotton and sugar. The town was founded as a military base in the 17th century,

largely to counter any English attacks. La Trinité is at the heart of the Caravelle peninsula, a major nature reserve with good walking and fine views from the highest point on the peninsula. Fishermens' houses are still in evidence, as is the

◀ Expect to rub shoulders with some sailing giants

▼ You can still catch glimpses of the old La Trinité-sur-Mer

The essentials:

FUEL Motor the length of the marina until the smaller half of the marina is on your starboard side. Ahead of you, to the left, will be the fuel berth.

REPAIRS Every imaginable marine repair service is available here. Many of the services seem to be gathered around the N end of the marina and further beyond the bridge. With such a wide range of services available, it might be best to seek advice from the capitainerie. Many yacht services are located in the Zone Artisanale (25 min walk to the N, 5 min by taxi).

CHANDLERY USHIP, 43 Cours des Quais (2 min walk) is N from the capitainerie.

LAUNDRY There is a laundry ashore close to K pontoon.

HIRE Cycle hire: some cycles are available at the capitainerie or try Le Trinitain, 44 Cours des Quais (2 min walk) – next to the chandlery, which offers electric bikes.

influence left by Trinidad's inhabitants during the days of the sugar trade.

THINGS TO SEE AND DO

There are two small beaches to the south of the marina (10 min walk), but the largest, **Plage de Kervillen**, is on the opposite side of the peninsula (30 min walk).

The town of **Carnac** (1 hr walk, 10 min by taxi) can make for a good day out if you are seeking ancient history.

The **Standing Stones of Carnac** have a high reputation and were erected in the Neolithic period from 4500 BCE to 3300 BCE. The reason for the stones and their layouts has led to much speculation; one of the more fanciful suggests that they were Roman soldiers turned to stone by Merlin. Free access to the stones.

FOOD AND SHOPPING

● **Carrefour City**, 1 Place Du Voulien (3 min walk inland from the capitainerie).
● **L'Épicerie du Port** (deli), 24 Cours des Quais (3 min walk).
● **Biscuiterie La Trinitaine**, 13 Cours des Quais (2 min walk), for everything biscuity in Brittany at this shop and factory.

- The **European flat oyster** is the speciality here and is rich in iodine.
- **Market** day is every Tuesday and Friday, Place du Voulien (10 min walk). The fish market – in the same building as the capitainerie – is open every day.

FURTHER AFIELD

The nearest train station in at Auray, Place Raoul Dautry (12 min by taxi).

Bus service No 1 (stops at the marina) goes to Auray (1 hr 15 min journey) and Vannes (1 hr 32 min journey) heading N, and S to Quiberon (57 min journey).

Tourist information

On the waterfront at 30 Cours des Quais (3 min walk N from the capitainerie)
Web: www.baiedequiberon.bzh/la-trinite-sur-mer
Tel: +33 2 44 84 56 56

▲ Step outside the marina for a glimpse of unspoilt Brittany

◄ The ancient stones at Carnac are impressive and worth the trip

PORT DU CROUESTY

PORT HALIGUEN 8NM, **ÎLE HOËDIC** 9NM, **LE CROISIC** 23NM

This substantial marina, said to be the largest in Brittany (1,500 berths), stands guard over the entrance to the Morbihan, an inland sea of over 60 islands and unlimited cruising and anchoring opportunities. This is *not* a quiet, out-of-the-way kind of place. Expect night clubs in this somewhat manufactured, modern resort. It is said that the inland sea was created by the tears of fairies. One suspects a sighting of this marina might have them crying all over again.

▼ The large and complex marina at Port du Crouesty

NAVIGATION

The marina is easy to approach and safe in all weathers. Inside, you'll find a large marina spilt into six smaller ones. If you're lucky, you may be met by a launch (usually good English) who will direct you – most visitor berths are on the S side. The capitainerie is also here. Don't worry unduly about ending up on the 'wrong' side, the harbour launch (VHF9) often ferries people from one side to the other, saving a considerable walk if you are shopping.

OVERVIEW

This is a convenient place but lacking in any Breton atmosphere you care to

The essentials:

(Note: no walking distances are given as it will greatly depend on which quarter of this sprawling marina you happen to be berthed in.)

FUEL At the foot of the tall white tower that forms the leading light.

REPAIRS You can get all repairs done here. 60T Travelift, 30T crane and storage ashore.

CHANDLERY There are numerous chandlers along the quayside that will be able to deal with most requests.

LAUNDRY On the marina, to be found SE of the visitors' basin. Also at Intermarché supermarket, which is at the head on the most northerly basin.

▼ Crouesty – the nearby coastline makes for a good escape from the marina

name. It's best to accept you are in a boat park and then your expectations will not disappoint. There is a pleasant beach close by and many opportunities for shopping therapy, and plenty of holiday atmosphere. There is also a little history to be enjoyed on its doorstep (see below).

THINGS TO SEE AND DO

On the S side of the marina entrance is **Notre-Dame du Crouesty**, 2 Vge de Pêcheurs, a chapel built in the 19th century. It follows on from many previous chapels in that location dating back to 565 when the body of St Gildas (see Auray) was found on a boat, aground on the rocks, but perfectly preserved despite having been at sea for three months. Every year on 15 August, a mass is celebrated here in memory of all lost sailors.

▲ A part of Brittany deeply rich in ancient history – the Cairn Petit Mont

Follow the coastal path a little further and you will come to the Cairn Petit Mont, an ancient tumulus topped by a prehistoric cairn. Access is possible to the cairn and its 6,000-year-old paintings.

There are good walks all along the coastal path, and on the beach to the S, where you will find windsurfing/paddleboarding etc.

FOOD AND SHOPPING
● The nearest village is Bourg d'Arzon (20 min walk northwards), which has a baker and usual supplies.
● There is a convenient supermarket on the marina – Intermarché SUPER on the N side.
● Monday morning market in the village.

FURTHER AFIELD
Nearest train station is at Vannes, ave. Favrel et Lincy, via bus No 24 (1 hr).

Trains from Vannes to Rennes (approx. 1 hr). Connections from there to Paris and all parts of Brittany. Trains from Rennes to St Malo (approx. 1 hr) for a ferry connection to the UK.

Tourist information
In the NE corner of the marina.
Web: www.morbihan.com
Tel: +33 2 97 53 69 69

AURAY

▶ The old port of St Goustan, seen from the heights of Auray

VANNES 16NM, BELLE-ÎLE 23NM, CROISIC 30NM, PORT HALIGUEN 17NM

Of the two towns in the Morbihan with facilities for yachts, Auray, at the head of a long (7NM) and winding river, offers you the chance of a more peaceful time when compared with Vannes to the E. It boasts good communications, so is useful for crew changing. However, there are two snags: there's no marina and there's a bridge with a limited air draft to negotiate. Nevertheless, a charming old town, which could easily have been created by Disney, awaits you.

NAVIGATION

Auray lies at the head of a river that needs careful attention as the flow can be strong and there are numerous islands. The major difficulty is the bridge; you must do careful calculations to ensure you can get under. I shall leave it to you and your pilot book and wish you well, noting that there are tidal gauges either side of the river. You might see a marina, but be aware this dries completely. Mooring is on trots between buoys.

OVERVIEW

Think of this almost as two towns. There's the lower part, St Goustan, where you find the harbour. Then climb the hill to the upper town, the focus of which is the church dedicated to St Gildas. Gildas the Wise was a

The essentials:

(Note: walking distances taken from the capitainerie.)

AMENITIES The capitainerie is to starboard side heading upriver, halfway between the two bridges, 24 Quai Benjamin Franklin. There is a permanent crane on the shore close by.

FUEL No fuel berth.

REPAIRS There are no repair facilities, or chandlery, in the town itself. At Port du Parun, halfway up the river on the E side, is a boatyard, Le Borgne (tidal access only) – all repair skills here. Otherwise, Port du Crouesty is your best bet.

FACILITIES Showers are behind the capitainerie.

LAUNDRY If not found at the harbour, try Ty'laverie, 7 ave. Maréchal Foch (15 min walk).

6th-century monk from Scotland, a literary figure and historian recording the history of the Britons in pre-Saxon times. He established a monastery in Brittany and his many followers came here to be taught by him.

Once a major trading port, Auray traded wine and grain from here. The streets and houses, some from between the 16th and 18th centuries, add great atmosphere. They call this the 'picture perfect' town and it is difficult to argue. Expect Breton music on summer evenings.

THINGS TO SEE AND DO

Start at the Place de la Republique (12 min walk), which is at the heart of the upper town, and stroll from there to find plentiful shops and some of the best atmosphere. Adjoining the Hôtel de Ville is the covered market (see below).

St Goustan (5 min walk), a compact gathering of ancient buildings, is the

old port area on the same side of the river as the capitainerie. Cobbled streets, quayside, cafés and restaurants. Street entertainment in the high season and flea markets. Hunt down the backstreet crêperies. This place has long attracted artists and sculptors.

The 18th-century **Hôtel de Ville**, 100 Place de la République (12 min walk) stands proud above the town and was completed in 1782.

Église St-Gildas, 7 Place Gabriel Deshayes (15 min walk). There's beautiful stained-glass work in this 17th-century church housing a major altarpiece and a 16th-century statue (recently restored) of a reclining Christ.

FOOD AND SHOPPING

- **Aldi, Monoprix, Super U** and **E. Leclerc** all have branches in Auray (walking time varies depending on which you visit).
- **Market** day is Monday morning in the town centre, Place de la République

(12 min walk) and is said to be one of the best in Brittany; 400 traders in high season.

- There is an **organic market** on Place Notre Dame (20 min walk) on Thursday 1700–2000 (25 stalls).
- The **municipal market hall**, next to the Hôtel de Ville, 100 Place de la République (12 min walk), is open every day of the week from 0800–1300.

FURTHER AFIELD

There is an SNCF station at Auray, Place Raoul Dautry (10 min by taxi), NE of the town.

Trains to Quimper (1 hr) and Vannes (10 min). Also, the Tire-Bouchon seasonal line, which runs S to Quiberon. Connections to all parts of northern France from Rennes.

Buses start from the SNCF station (also with a stop in the centre) to Vannes, Quiberon and Carnac.

If planning a crew change: from the Roscoff ferry, take the bus to Morlaix, then train to Auray via Brest (5 hr) or take a taxi (2 hr 20 min). From the St Malo ferry, train to Rennes, then onwards to Auray (3 hr 15 min).

The nearest airport is Lorient (LRT), but there are possibly more flights from the UK to Nantes, then direct train to Auray from Nantes' centre (3 hr including shuttle from the airport).

Tourist information
20 rue du Lait (15 min walk)
Web: www.baiedequiberon.bzh/auray
Tel: +33 2 44 84 56 56

▲ The imposing town hall takes centre stage in Auray

◄ **1–4** Timbered houses and cobbled streets – the best of Breton atmosphere in St Goustan; **5** The marina is found downstream from St Goustan, a short walk from the old town

► (*Overleaf*) The old port of St Goustan still shines in the sun!

VANNES

▶ In Vannes, the ramparts public gardens are perfectly manicured

BELLE-ÎLE 24NM, **LORIENT** 40NM, **LE CROISIC** 33NM, **AURAY** 16NM

A walled city, half-timbered houses and ramparts, all in a town that manages to have a strong sense of tradition, but at the same time prosperity as well. It is described as the 'pearl' of the Morbihan. The liveliest part of town is the Place Gambetta, at the head of the long, thin marina. You could eat and drink yourself into a blissful state here.

NAVIGATION

You need a strong understanding of the sweeping Morbihan tides. Approaching the marina, you must first negotiate a swing bridge before arriving at a tidal gate (no lock). Daylight hours only. Outbound boats have priority. The marina is safe in any weather.

OVERVIEW

Having been founded over 2,000 years ago, Vannes became a cathedral city in the 5th century and by the Middle Ages was one of the most important towns in Brittany. In the 17th century, convents grew up and the silting of the all-important harbour (vital to the wine-growing trade) caused new quays to be built and the straightening of the river channel. When the railway came in 1862, industry and an increasing population followed.

These days, you'll find it a place for artists and drinkers who enjoy trendy bars, and good food at every turn. The quay that runs alongside the W of the marina is Quai Eric Tabarly, and on the E, Quai Bernard Moitessier – so you are in good sailing company.

▼ Half-timber and bright paintwork sets the atmosphere of Vannes

THINGS TO SEE AND DO

Walk the **ramparts**. Some of these date from the 3rd century AD and are among the best preserved in Brittany. Start at the Porte St Vincent Ferrier (a Spanish monk and the town's patron saint) and the walk will take you under an hour.

Château Gaillard, 2 rue Noé (15 min walk) is a small archaeological museum – coins, axe heads, religious panels and the excavation of the local megalithic stones. Terrific setting in a tall, thin, 15th-century manor house that leans against the ramparts – the fireplaces are superb. On the third floor, note the ceiling in the shape of a boat. Joint tickets can be bought for the La Cohue art collection (see below).

▼ Good shore life at the head of the marina in Vannes

The essentials:

(Note: walking distances are from the capitainerie.)

AMENITIES The capitainerie is on the starboard side as you enter (good restaurant above).

FUEL There is no fuel berth here.

REPAIRS There is a boatyard with lifting facilities on the E side between the tidal gate and the marina. Chantier Naval Le Pennec, 62 rue du Commerce (7 min walk).

CHANDLERY Chandlery and repairs at Chantier Naval Caudard, 26 allée Loic Caradec (25 min walk) on the W bank of the river, below the swing bridge.

FACILITIES Showers, toilets and laundry are in the capitainerie, and are of a high standard.

HIRE Cycle hire: Veloc'Ouest by Golfe Hôtel (20 min walk), SW from the marina. Electric bikes can be hired from the rail station (see below).

La Cohue, 15 Place St Pierre (18 min walk). Find this museum opposite the cathedral in a building that was once the seat of the Breton parliament and a covered market. It's now a museum of the fine arts majoring on contemporary artists from the late-19th through 20th centuries – you may need an eye for modern art to enjoy some of the works.

Parc du Golfe, rue Daniel Gilard (20 min walk), is the joining point if you want to take a boat trip.

Vannes Aquarium, 21 rue Daniel Gilard (20 min walk). Excellent aquarium with a tropical fish collection and butterflies in huge numbers under a glass dome. Fresh and saltwater species, sharks and crocodiles. A touch tank that children will enjoy.

Beyond here is the Plage de Conleau (26 min walk), which is Vannes' only

▲ A safe and secure berth in one of Brittany's finest towns

beach. Between the two you have a memorable day out for children.

Vedettes du Golfe, 8 Allée Loic Caradec (15 min walk) on the W side of the marina.

If you don't fancy weaving your way round the islands of the Morbihan, there are boat trips a plenty to choose from.

FOOD AND SHOPPING
● Monoprix, Place Joseph le Brix (17 min walk).
● There are two branches of Carrefour City, pretty much the same distance from the marina office: 10–12 rue Hoche (20 min walk) and

23 rue Robert Schumann (25 min walk).
- There seems to be a **market** of one sort or another almost every day of the week, two of which are indoors, and one outdoors.
- The indoor fish market on **Place de la Poissonerie** (8 min walk) takes place on Tuesday, Wednesday, Friday and Saturday, 0700–1300.
- **Halle de Lices** (10 min walk), on the square of the same name, offers fruit, veg, cheese, meat and more, and is open Tuesday to Sunday 0800–1400.
- **Open-air market** at Place des Lices (10 min walk), which was once a venue for jousting tournaments, takes place on Wednesday and Saturday mornings.

FURTHER AFIELD
The SNCF station, ave. Favrel et Lincy (30 min walk) is N from the marina. From here, trains to Paris (2 hr 30 min) and to London (6 hr 30 min) via Paris and Eurostar. Trains to Cherbourg for a ferry connection (6 hr 30 min). Trains to Roscoff via Morlaix, then a bus connection Morlaix to Roscoff (6 hr).

Vannes to St Malo by car (2 hr) with ferry connections to the UK (Plymouth or Poole).

Nearest airports at Rennes (1 hr 30 min) and Nantes (1 hr 45 min).

Local bus services are operated by Kiceo and Vélocéo.

Tourist information: Quai Eric Tabarly (10 min walk) on the W side of the marina
Web: www.morbihan.com
Tel: +33 2 97 47 24 34

▼ It's such a perfectly traditional place, it almost could have stepped out of a Disney film

THE VILAINE RIVER

(TO THE RIVER ENTRANCE) MORBIHAN ENTRANCE 21NM, ÎLE HOËDIC 20NM, PORT HALIGUEN 25NM, ST NAZAIRE 30NM

Protected from the sea by a barrage, the Vilaine River has a maintained depth and little tidal flow – it's a bit like sailing on a lake and in fresh water – you'll float slightly lower in the water. This river is much favoured by UK yachts. There are two marinas near the barrage, a medieval town upstream at La Roche-Bernard, and for those who wish to venture inland there is the town of Redon, where the river meets the Brittany inland canal system. To go any further requires the removal of your mast.

NAVIGATION
The river seaward of the barrage is shallow and strong winds against an ebb tide will kick up quite a sea. Spot the lock by the control tower nearby.

It's a decent-sized lock but quite busy in the season and can be turbulent if there is a large rise and fall, and lifejackets *must* be worn. There are two marinas just inside: Arzal to the N, and Camoël to the S.

Keep an eye on your sounder as you go further upriver, especially on the corners. There is 3m (9.8ft) of water to La Roche-Bernard where Le Port Neuf is the second marina on the starboard side (the first is mostly for locals). At Redon, entry to the marina is via a lock – visitor berths are to your left as you enter. The river authorities are very keen on their environmental stewardship and promote the use of holding tanks.

▼ Two large, but hardly atmospheric marinas, at Arzal

▲ Good shelter beneath the town of La Roche-Bernard

▶ The lock that allows entrance to the river can be full to bursting in high season

ARZAL MARINA

There are 1,200 berths but little atmosphere – it's a boat park with an isolated feel. There are two restaurants.

FOOD AND SHOPPING
● For restricted groceries, the village of Arzal is 2km (1.2 miles) from the marina.

> **The essentials:**
>
> FUEL Fuel and pump-out are available.
>
> REPAIRS Offers all marine specialities, from engineers, sailmaker, lift out, electrics and all repairs, close to the marina.
>
> CHANDLERY Large UShip chandlery, Port de Plaisance.
>
> HIRE Cycle hire: at the capitainerie.

CAMOËL MARINA

On the S side, this is quieter and with fewer facilities. To use this marina, you must check in at Arzal (same management). No fuel, repairs or chandlery.

> **The essentials:**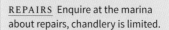
>
> FUEL No fuel berth at this marina – Arzal is the nearest.
>
> REPAIRS Enquire at the marina about repairs, chandlery is limited.
>
> FACILITIES Showers and toilets can be found close to the harbour office.

▼ The Vilaine River, cut off from the sea by the lock at Arzal, can make for peaceful cruising

LE PORT NEUF

This is the main marina at La Roche-Bernard, which is by far the most interesting stopping place on this river. You may be able to get basic repairs done here.

La Roche-Bernard is a delightful medieval town and will be the highlight of cruising this part of France. It was once an important trading port where salt, corn, wine and chestnut wood were shipped from. However, it fell into disuse with the coming of the railway. It was originally a Viking settlement,

largely due to its strategic position. You'll find potters and artists and can buy local honey and generally soak up the medieval feel of the town.

THINGS TO SEE AND DO

Musée de la Vilaine Maritime, 6 rue du Ruicard (5 min walk from Le Port Neuf). The museum tells the story of the 17th-century warship building and the maritime history of this once important trading river. It is housed in the Basses-Fosses castle.

The **promenade** beside the river provides a showcase for intriguing sculptures, among them a one-third scale model of the 18th-century galleon, *La Couronne* – she was built here in 1634.

Flotille Traditionnelle de la Basse Vilaine is based in La Roche-Bernard – a group of vintage boatowners who offer river trips.

To enjoy the town, and its cafés and bars, start in the centre at the **Place du Bouffay** (10 min walk).

> ### The essentials:
>
> **FUEL** There is no fuel berth here.
>
> **REPAIRS** A local boatyard with chandlery and engine repairs.
>
> **FACILITIES** Showers close to harbour office.
>
> **LAUNDRY** May be possible at an adjoining campsite.

FOOD AND SHOPPING

- Carrefour Express, 5 Place du Puits (10 min walk).
- Carrefour Drive Nivillac (larger supermarket), blvd de Bretagne, not far from the Carrefour Express (above) (12 min walk).
- Joyeux Marché (organic fruit and veg), 13 rue du Dr Cornudet (5 min walk).
- Market day is in the centre of town on Thursday mornings and is highly recommended.

FURTHER AFIELD

It is a 40 min bus ride to Redon (route 10) where trains connect to Rennes (40 min), from where you can find connections to all parts of Brittany.

The airport at Rennes (1 hr 30 min by taxi) is to the SW of the city. Flights to Paris (1 hr) and onward connections to the UK.

If sailing upriver to Redon, you will find it to be a major commercial centre but at its heart it is still a town of canals and locks with a safe and pleasant marina at its centre. It is famous for its Benedictine Abbey, the

▲ Plenty of arts and crafts on offer at La Roche-Bernard

most important in Brittany. It is a major transport hub: six major roads meet here, as well as canals and the railway line to Rennes. There is still evidence of its heyday in the houses once belonging to merchants and sea captains.

Tourist information: 14 rue du Dr Cornudet (5 min walk)
Web: www.damgan-larochebernard-tourisme.com
Tel: +33 2 97 41 11 32

▼ The considerable tidal barrier at Arzal

PAYS DE LA LOIRE

PIRIAC-SUR-MER
► LA ROCHELLE

A BIT OF A NEWCOMER is this district, having been created as recently as the 1950s. Its name is derived from the Loire Valley, which is a UNESCO World Heritage site.

In the Loire Valley, vegetables, fruit and wine are the major crops. This is good grazing country, and although the coastline is often low-lying, expect to see cows grazing to feed the hugely important dairy industry. Consequently, the region is known for its dairy-based foods, which include Port Salut cheese, beurre blanc sauce – a French classic of shallots, white wine, vinegar and butter enriched with cream – and the fleur de sel, which is salt harvested from salt pans found to the S of the region. Crêperies are abundant.

That said, tourists are also hugely important and there are many popular resorts and harbours. The 27km (17 mile)-long strip of coast S of the Loire is known as the 'Côte de Jade' because of the apparent green colour of the sea.

The Vendée is a department within the Pays de la Loire, probably best known for the singlehanded round-the-world yacht race, the Vendée Globe, which departs every four years from Les Sables-d'Olonne.

If you really want a break from the boat and are prepared to travel inland, the Puy du Fou theme park has been voted 'the best in the world' – gladiators, Vikings, medieval knights, birds of prey and spectacular sound and light shows are on offer. It can be found inland of Les Sables-d'Olonne (1 hr 15 min by car).

▼ Watch the sun set over the old harbour of La Rochelle

PIRIAC-SUR-MER

ST NAZAIRE 33NM, **ARZAL** 10NM, **MORBIHAN ENTRANCE** 19NM

The coastline here is called the Côte d'Amour and you will certainly love it. Piriac-sur-Mer is small with a population of just over 2,000 people, and is not a sophisticated sort of place. It's somewhere to pause, take a breath and refresh yourself.

▲ There's no missing this harbour entrance

NAVIGATION

The approach dries and the depths, in places, are uncertain. Allow plenty of rise of tide. The marina is protected by a sill. If you're lucky, you'll be met by a marina launch. The capitainerie is on the S side of the marina (the tall, grey building with a prominent sign).

OVERVIEW

The town sits on the Guérande peninsula amidst a largely unspoilt landscape. The alleyways between the 17th-century houses can overflow with the scent of roses – it's a florally decorated kind of place. It inspired Flaubert and Zola and will probably charm you.

Although it's close to the dividing line between the Pays de la Loire and Brittany, the Breton feel of this place

▼ Piriac-sur-Mer is modest compared with some of the larger Breton marinas

▲ There's a peaceful atmosphere by the marina

is undeniable. The beaches stretch for several kilometres, but many have found it a joy to simply walk the cobbled streets and the half-timbered houses. After some of the glossier resorts of Brittany, this is a take-you-out-of-yourself kind of place.

THINGS TO SEE AND DO

The St Michel beach at Piriac (walk W from the marina for 8 min) is the most popular for families, with a beach club organising a full programme of activities. For a quieter time, this stretch of coastline offers coves and small beaches well away from the crowds.

▶ There's far less bustle here than in other parts of the region

Take the coastal footpath to the Castelli headland with terrific views along the way (45 min walk). Find walking routes at the tourist information (see below).

Piriac Adventure Tree Climbing, 2057 route de Mesquer (35 min walk) for a family day out with climbing and scrambling for all ages, starting at two years old. This was the first adventure park in Brittany. Bike hire is also found here, along with a picnic area.

The walled town of Guérande is a 25 min taxi ride away or 45 min by bus.

Explore arts and crafts, galleries and the famous salt ponds where 10,000 tons of salt a year are produced.

Almanzor Tomb is a remarkable lump of rock with an uncertain history. Much legend surrounds it, but I won't spoil it for you (30 min walk on the S side of the peninsula).

Maison du Patrimoine Heritage Centre, 3 Place Henri Vignioboul (5 min walk). Some 6,000 years of history is depicted here, including artists and writers, farming and sardine fishing.

FOOD AND SHOPPING

● Head S from the marina and you will soon find the heart of the village with **boulangerie, boucherie, pharmacie** and numerous **bars, cafés** and **restaurants**.

● **Carrefour City**, 2 rue du Vieux Moulin (10 min walk).

▲ Piriac is strong on Breton atmosphere, despite its proximity to Pays de la Loire

▼ Good beaches and rock scrambling close to the harbour

- There are **markets** of Monday, Wednesday and Saturday, Place Paul Vince (6 min walk) but in the high season only.

FURTHER AFIELD
Nearest railway station at Le Croisic (25 min by taxi) with trains to Paris (4–5 hr) and Nantes (1 hr 20 min).

For a day away from the boat, try La Baule, which is famous for villas, its casino and a sense of an exclusive resort with 9km (5.6 miles) of beach. Take No 4 bus from Piriac (56 min). There are also buses to Guérande (41 min).

Tourist information: 7 rue des Cap-Horniers (10 min walk)
Web: www.labaule-guerande.com/piriac-sur-mer.html
Tel: +33 2 40 24 34 44

▼ The essentials are close at hand

LA TURBALLE

▲ Fishing is the name of the game here

PIRIAC-SUR-MER 6NM, **LE CROISIC** 4NM, **ST NAZAIRE** 18NM, **ÎLE HOËDIC** 15NM

A working fishing port to which strings of high-rise flats have been added along the waterfront. It's a decent place, but not inspiring. It's a very popular tourist destination due to its lengthy (blue flag) beaches, the best being to the S.

NAVIGATION

There is access here at all tides, which makes it a convenient stopover, but perhaps not somewhere to linger. The marina is small and can be tightly packed in high season – expect rafting. Also, in high season, you might be unlucky and turned away. The capitainerie is on the mole on the S side of the harbour.

OVERVIEW

This town (created in 1865 from a collection of villages and hamlets) initially owed its prosperity to sardine fishing. It is still a major fishing centre, with anchovies and sardines being the main summer catches. The nearby marshes have a strong environmental draw and are a major part of the attraction of this area. The beaches have lifeguards in July and August. You will find leisure centres on all the major beaches.

THINGS TO SEE AND DO

The Fête de la Sardine is held in the fish market auction area (Port du pêche, 5 min walk) in July – obtain precise

▲ It's a modest town, but most supplies can be found here

The essentials: ⚓

FUEL On the harbour wall to the SW, or at garage a lengthy 20 min walk from marina (TotalEnergies, 20 rue de la Frégate).

REPAIRS A substantial Travelift can take all yachts and it is possible to arrange repairs here.

CHANDLERY 2 Quai St Jacques, opposite the marina (short walk).

LAUNDRY In the capitainerie building.

dates from tourist information (see below).

The tourist information will also advise on harbour visits, including the daily 0600 fish auction.

Cinéma Atlantic, Trescallan (30 min walk), will meet your big screen needs.

There is a naturist beach to the S at Pen Bron (35 min walk).

FOOD AND SHOPPING
● Boulangerie Pâtisserie Maleuvre Fabrice, 85 rue du Maréchal Juin (8 min walk).
● Les Artisans du Pain, 18 rue du Maréchal Leclerc (7 min walk).

● Carrefour City, rue de la Poste (10 min walk).
● Larger supermarket Super U et Drive, 2 rue des Pins (20 min walk).

FURTHER AFIELD
Nearest train station at La Baule-Escoublac (35 min by bus every 4 hr) with ten trains a day to Paris (approx. 3 hr). For connections to other parts of western France, change at Nantes.

Tourist information: Rue Charles de Gaulle (7 min walk)
Web: www.labaule-guerande.com/la-turballe.html
Tel: +33 2 40 24 34 44

▼ No danger of avoiding fish on every menu

LE CROISIC

ARZAL 30NM, **LE POULIGUEN** 9NM, **PORNIC** 25NM, **ST NAZAIRE** 20NM

It's a salty kind of place where the TGV from Paris arrives within spitting distance of the waterfront. The vast spread of mussel beds and salt pans are a sight to see, as is some of 16th-century merchant architecture with the stone hewn from the granite peninsula on which the town stands.

NAVIGATION

The entrance is long and narrow alongside a training wall with leading lines to help you. The marina dries, but deep yachts can take the ground on firm sand. There are moorings N of the marina, but the tides run strongly and anchoring space is limited – trip lines are needed. Tides can run at 4 knots off the fish market. The capitainerie is on the starboard side of the marina entrance.

OVERVIEW

Le Croisic owes its 16th-century foundation to the nearby salt flats from where salt was traded with the rest of north-west Europe in exchange for iron and coal. Fishing was always important but became a major industry in the 19th century when sardine canneries were established. At the same time, a new leisure activity emerged – sea bathing, which was the start of the

▼ Sit on the quayside and watch your boat settle at LW

▲ A long, winding and shallow approach

▶ A shallow harbour amidst the flat lands of the Loire

tourist invasion here.

While some harbours like to show off their bustling fish auction areas, here they prefer to close the doors to visitors. Although it is tempting to confine your walking to the lengthy waterfront, the historical centre based around the church is not to be missed.

The US Navy established an early naval air station here in order to operate seaplanes during the First World War.

THINGS TO SEE AND DO
Plage de Port Lin is the most popular family holiday beach (15 min walk S to the far side of the peninsula – part of the Côte Sauvage).

Oceanarium, ave. de St Goustan (25 min walk NW from the marina) is one of the largest private aquariums

The essentials:
FUEL No fuel berth here.

REPAIRS Marine engineers etc can be found in the industrial area E of the railway terminus. Substantial Travelift.

CHANDLERY Comptoir de la Mer, 1 rue du Mail de Broc (12 min walk seaward of the marina).

HIRE Cycle hire: Ty Vélo, by the railway station (5 min walk S from the harbour).

▼ Don't worry, you'll sink into very soft sand

Espace Escargots, 33 rue des Becs Sales (30 min walk), is great for those who appreciate the lifestyle of snails – it's a snail farm with an opportunity for tasting after your tour.

Annual **Fête de Mer** is held in mid-August.

On Monday evenings in July and August, street artists and musicians line the quays, accompanied by an evening **market**.

in France with more than 4,000 sea creatures spread across 56 tanks. It attracts a quarter of a million visitors a year.

Route des Coquillages (shellfish trail) – ask at tourist information (see below) for details of this guided tour.

FOOD AND SHOPPING

● The main shopping street is **Quai de la Petite Chambre**, and the town has no fewer than five Michelin-listed restaurants.

● **François & Rosalie Boulangerie**, 20 rue

▲ There's always a quiet street on which you can get away from the summer crowds

▶ Storms can roll in off the rich farming land inshore of Le Croisic

▼ (*Overleaf*) Le Croisic may be a small town, but it's got plenty of character

de la Marine (very close to the marina on the S side), is the closest bakery.

- Coccinelle Supermarché, Place Dinan (5 min walk) is close to the marina.
- There is a weekly **market** on Thursday and Saturday mornings (and Tuesdays in July and August) in the covered market, rue des Cordiers (8 min walk) and a Thursday open-air market in Place Dinan (7 min walk).
- For all kinds of **fishing tackle**, head to Place Donatien Lèpre (10 min walk).

FURTHER AFIELD

The town has its own SNCF station with a line from St Nazaire, which is an extension of the line from Tours.

The nearest airport is Nantes Atlantique (1 hr 20 min by taxi) or train to Nantes (1 hr 5 min), and taxi from there.

▲ With the 19th-century tourist invasion came the wealthy to build their villas

Tourist information

6 rue du Pilori (3 min walk)
Web: www.tourisme-lecroisic.fr
Tel: +33 2 40 23 00 70

LE POULIGUEN

LE CROISIC 12NM, **PORNICHET** 3NM, **LA TURBALLE** 13NM, **BELLE-ÎLE** 30NM

You get two places for the price of one here: Le Pouliguen to port as you enter and Benoît to starboard, although both are commonly grouped together under the Pouliguen name. They are situated on the W end of the Bay of La Baule, which is described as 'one of the most beautiful in the world'. There is a feeling here of being in a smart, wealthy resort.

NAVIGATION

Some careful navigation is needed to avoid rocky reefs in Baie du Pouliguen, then it's a buoyed channel into a river after crossing a sill. This river feeds some of the salt marshes. Streams up to 4 knots. You can anchor seaward of the sill to wait for the tide, or a waiting buoy may be available. The bureau du port is on the E side on entry – a grey granite villa with a welcoming yacht club.

OVERVIEW

You are now in the Loire-Atlantique district, leaving Brittany behind, though the Breton language has been maintained here. It was certainly the commonest language in parts of the town as late as the end of the 19th century. Fishing and the movement of salt were the main industries before tourism, and the grand houses built for

merchants and shipowners still stand. Benoît takes its name from the Benoît brothers, who established fish canning factories here in the 1830s. Industry took something of a back seat with the arrival of the railway in 1879, bringing Parisian tourists into town.

The sandy beach at Le Pouliguen, Plage du Nau, is reckoned to be the better of the two. If you are a scrambler, then the rocky coves further along provide good exploration, with caves said to house pixies.

Note that the marina is on the E bank of the river, and the best shopping in Le Pouliguen is on the W bank – you will have to walk up to the bridge to cross the river. A ferry runs 0900–2300 and saves a walk. The area inland of the marina is largely (expensive) residential.

▲ A lengthy and narrow approach, but note the extensive beaches to the E

The essentials:

FUEL By credit card on the marina – look for the ferry berth.

REPAIRS There are repair facilities here, with a chandlery close by the marina. Check first at the capitainere if seeking advice.

LAUNDRY Use Laverie Speed Queen, 22 rue Général Leclerc (8 min walk – across the bridge).

HIRE Cycle hire: bikeEvasion, 9 rue Général Leclerc (8 min walk).

▶ The bridge that connects the marina to the main shopping areas

◀ The marina is on the E side, in Benoît, strictly speaking

▲ Good timing is needed at the fuel berth

THINGS TO SEE AND DO

This is a not a place for touristy attractions, but rather a town with an enjoyable and relaxed atmosphere with splendid beaches close by.

FOOD AND SHOPPING

● The main shopping area is in the old town. Cross the bridge and turn left for plentiful shopping, restaurants, cafés etc (10 min walk).

● For bread and patisserie somewhat closer, cross the bridge and walk directly ahead (5 min), where you will find a bakery (on the right-hand side), Le Fournil de mon Pére, and 'artisan' pizza opposite a butcher.

● For high-class groceries, try Le Délice du Pouliguen, 5 rue du Centre (10 min walk), close by the main church, Église St Nicolas.

● Lidl, 38 ave. de Llantwit Major (10 min walk) – across the bridge and keep going.

● For major provisioning, Intermarché Hyper et Drive, 20 rue de Cornen (20 min walk/5 min by taxi).

● The market, Marché des Halles du Pouliguen, is open Tuesday, Friday and Saturday (across the bridge, first left, 5 min walk). It sells oysters, cheese butchery, poultry – a food-lover's heaven. Bars and cafés are also close by.

FURTHER AFIELD

There is an SNCF station here (Place de la Gare, 15 min walk) with trains

▼ A promise of family fun on a vibrant quayside

▼ A cautious approach to navigation is needed here

to Le Croisic (37 min) and Nantes (1 hr 24 min) with connections from there to all parts of northern France, including Paris (3 hr 30 min).

Buses start from outside the railway station to Nantes (1 hr 24 min), Pornichet (1 hr 30 min) and St Nazaire (1 hr 3 min).

Tourist information: Locate the two bridges and find the office halfway between them on the W bank (5 min walk) Web: www.labaule-guerande.com/le-pouliguen.html Tel: +33 2 40 24 34 44

◄ The market is probably the best place to stock up with fresh food

PORNICHET

▲ Once highly fashionable, but more family friendly now

LE POULIGUEN 3NM, BELLE-ÎLE 30NM, PORT HALIGUEN 35NM, PORNIC 20NM

Pornichet more or less merges with La Baule, which is one of the most visited resorts in this part of France. It features endless sandy beaches all backed by apparently endless high-rise apartment blocks. Go inland to see the massive villas built in the belle époque era. There's good walking and cycling (35km/21.8 miles of paths) if you tire of sand. It's a great place for children – it has a 'Kid Resort' label – and there are plenty of ways to pass the time if you're waiting for weather.

NAVIGATION

You can enter this marina in any weather and at any state of tide. It is vast, with more than 1,000 berths, so expect much walking. English is spoken in the capitainerie and ice is available. It is somewhat of a blind entrance so a good lookout is needed for emerging boats. Some of a pontoon labelling is a bit opaque, so call CH9 and you might get help from a launch.

OVERVIEW

This has been a fashionable resort since the 19th century, hence the substantial villas you will find if you wander into 'Old' Pornichet. The present town wasn't created until 1900 and before that it was considered a hamlet on the far outskirts of St Nazaire. Like many resorts along this coast, it owes its

prosperity to the arrival of the railway line from Paris.

There are three beaches: the main one is plage des Libraires (booksellers' beach), located along blvd des Océanides, and this adjoins the large beach of La Baule. You'll find another beach, Bonne Source, if you head off in the direction of St Nazaire. The walk across the bridge from the marina and past the apartment blocks is uninspiring but the town is regarded as one of the most floral in the region.

▼ It's a huge marina – put on your walking shoes

The essentials:

FUEL Payment by credit card, located on pontoon P.

REPAIRS 25T Travelift. Outboard dealerships, chandlery – all on the marina.

LAUNDRY Laverie du Marché, 9 ave. Gambetta (15 min walk).

HIRE Cycle hire: Cycles Bay, 74 ave. du Général de Gaulle (20 min walk). Ride All Pornichet, 52 blvd des Océanides (20 min walk).

THINGS TO SEE AND DO

Casino Pornichet, 93 blvd des Océanides (25 min walk) – gaming tables with blackjack and roulette, slot machines, computer games and poker. The food is said to be good and enjoyable to eat while overlooking the bay. The minimum entrance age is 18 years.

Hippodrome, the Pornichet racecourse, 3 ave. de l'Hippodrome (20 min walk). There's just a 5 euro entrance fee and it has a restaurant and cycle parking and children's events on race days. This is a major horse racing venue and horses and jockeys will come from all parts of Europe. It was rebuilt in 2011, giving the place a modern feel. Sand tracks allow racing all year round in all weathers. There has been racing here since 1907 and it has grown into a popular tourist destination.

Les Renc'Arts festival runs from mid-July to mid-August on two nights

▲ Substantial hotels are still part of the Pornichet scene

of the week: Tuesday for street arts, Thursday for music. There are games and shows, and plenty to entertain children.

Club de l'Albatros is on the beach, opposite 132 blvd des Océanides (25 min walk). Everything is aimed at children here – sailing school, swimming, bouncy castle, trampolines, swings.

The magnificent **villas of Pornichet**

▼ Miles of top-class beaches – pity about the blocks of flats

deserve a lingering look – for guided tours, ask at Le Bidule, 122 ave. Mazy (25 min walk), which is a wine cellar where sooner or later everyone seems to meet up. They serve only bidule or muscat. Bring your own snacks. It closes around 2100 – an eccentric kind of place. Start your evening here and then move on.

FOOD AND SHOPPING

There are bars, cafés and restaurants aplenty on the marina, but you have to go elsewhere for bread and groceries:
- Intermarché SUPER, ave. du Baulois (25 min walk).
- SPAR (nearest supermarket, just over the bridge), 16 blvd de la Republique (10 min walk).
- Boulangerie à la Lune, 164 ave. du Général de Gaulle (10 min walk).
- Fromagerie Maison Heude, Place de Maréchal Joffre (12 min walk) for a stunning selection of cheeses.

▲ The splendid market hall, close to the marina

- Les Halles de Pornichet, Place du Marché (12 min walk) – a stunning indoor and outdoor market Wednesday and Saturday. Best market for value.

FURTHER AFIELD

The SNCF station is about 2km (1.2 miles) from the marina, found by walking N up the ave de Général de Gaulle (30 min walk).

Nearest airport at Nantes – 50 min by train to Nantes, then 25 min on the airport bus.

There is a bus service (L13) to St Nazaire (40 min). The bus station is at the railway station.

Tourist information: 3 blvd de la République (10 min walk)
Web: www.pornichet.fr
Tel: +33 2 40 61 33 33

ST NAZAIRE

▼ A welcome beach on the western fringes of a highly industrialised city – 'Mr Hulot's Beach'

BELLE-ÎLE 40NM, **ÎLE D'YEU** 35NM, **LA TURBALLE** 23NM

This is hardly a go-to destination, and most cruisers would think it was best avoided. In fact, yachts are discouraged from entering. There are no real facilities for yachts, and no infrastructure, although it is possible to lie in one of the basins, mindful that this is a commercial/industrial area and you may be asked to move at short notice.

NAVIGATION

This needs attention and careful pilotage to avoid impeding the movement of shipping in the main approach channels. Monitor VHF 14. All yacht moorings require access through locks. Tidal flow in the river can be very strong. Head for the Bassin de Saint-Nazaire and berth along the W wall.

OVERVIEW

A plan was developed in 2019 to build a marina here, but it was abandoned, although there is talk (2022) of a resurrection of the project. The best advice is to moor up in Pornichet and get the train if you develop a thirst for city life.

▼ The imposing bridge across the Loire River gives large ships access to this major port

Despite being set among some of the finest beaches on the French Biscay coast, this is an unapologetically industrial city. It is renowned for its shipbuilding – the *Queen Mary 2* was constructed here. It is also a base for one of Europe's Airbus factories.

In the first half of the 19th century, this was little more than a village, and it owes its growth as a maritime centre to the transatlantic liners that left from here, starting in 1862, to South America. Later, in the Second World War, it became a German submarine base and eventually the French HQ of the German fleet. It had huge strategic significance for the Germans as this was the only Atlantic-facing port that could house the giant battleships *Bismarck* and *Tirpitz*.

This made St Nazaire a prime target for the Allies, who fought to destroy not only the submarines but also the huge shipyards that gave support to the German fleet. St Nazaire is reckoned to be the most damaged of all the French cities in the Second World War. The legendary submarine pens, however, remained undamaged and are still standing to this day, expert opinion being that they can be considered 'indestructible'. Should the marina development take place, it will likely be alongside the pens, which are now home to shops, cafés and workshops.

THINGS TO SEE AND DO

If you decide to take the train from Pornichet, here are a couple of maritime things worth seeing in St Nazaire. Distances are given as walking times from the railway station.

The submarine *Espadon* and Ecomusée, ave. de St Hubert (30 min walk). This was the first French submarine to dive beneath the Arctic

The essentials:

FACILITIES Water and electricity on the pontoons.

No other facilities available for yachts until marina development takes place.

ice field and is part of Ecomusée, which takes you through the maritime and industrial history of St Nazaire and the surrounding area. Expect ship models, seaplanes, paintings and a wealth of marine artefacts. Labels are in French but an English information leaflet is available.

Escal'Atlantic, 16 blvd de la Légion d'Honneur (20 min walk). Located within the submarine base is a total transatlantic liner experience with audiovisual and interactive display and liner artefacts. Atmospheric and informative. Voyage through the history of the great liners.

STX shipyard tour (20 min walk). This is where the world's largest cruise ship, the *Harmony of the Seas*, was built in 2016. The bus tour lasts about 2 hr and starts from the submarine base. There's one trip a week in July and August, in English.

Airbus tour (20 min walk). This tour takes you through the St Nazaire Airbus factory and starts from the submarine base on Wednesday and Friday. Booking is needed 48 hr in

▲ Traditional fishing huts line the river, away from the industrial face of St Nazaire

advance and ID must be shown.

There are cruises from the harbour (check location with tourist information, see below), which can take you away from the city to view the craggy coastline and its beaches. There's also a night-time cruise so you can take in the twinkle of the lighthouses and navigation marks.

FOOD AND SHOPPING
● There is a supermarket close to the submarine pens: Carrefour Drive, Bd de la Légion d'Honneur (10 min walk).

FURTHER AFIELD
The SNCF station is at Place Pierre Semard, (20 min walk) with trains to Paris (3 hr 30 min journey) and Nantes (37 min journey).

Tourist information: 12 blvd de la Légion d'Honneur (20 min walk)
Web: www.saint-nazaire-tourisme.com
Tel: +33 2 40 22 40 65

PORNIC

ÎLE D'YEU 40NM, **LES SABLES-D'OLONNE** 65NM, **PORNICHET** 18NM,
LE CROISIC 27NM

Brittany is now behind you, if you're heading southwards. The sun will be higher in the sky, the days warmer. It is somewhere around here that you will start to feel a sense of the Mediterranean climate being not too far away. This is the 'Jade Coast' and Pornic is described as its jewel. The marina is large and modern, but the old harbour houses fishing and traditional boats. Combined with stylish villas and good shoreside walking, there is plenty about this place to make it an attractive, relaxing and possibly expensive stopover.

NAVIGATION
The marina is easy to enter and is dredged to 2m (6.6ft) but can silt up, so avoid dead LW, especially at springs. Also avoid the old harbour, which dries. The reception pontoon is well marked.

OVERVIEW
Expect flights of steps linking narrow streets snaking between traditional fishermen's houses. Also expect some stunning houses that smack of great wealth. Tourism developed here with the coming of the railway. The train

▼ Some maritime tradition survives in the inner harbour beyond the marina

▼ Moorings for locals with the substantial marina beyond

brought with it the artist Renoir and the writer Flaubert. Albert Camus, philosopher and writer, visited too and wrote, 'Charm is a way of getting the answer "Yes" without asking a clear question'. You too will be charmed by Pornic, whatever its question might have been. It's a 15 min walk into the town and a bit of steep hiking to get up to the old town.

THINGS TO SEE AND DO

If you're seeking **beaches**, there is one close to the W end of the marina. Take the shoreside road, blvd de l'Océan, to find a wide choice of small, secluded beaches, and at the same time enjoy the impressive houses and their wooded gardens overlooking the sea.

To find the **old town**, head for the prominent church spire, Église de Ste

The essentials:

FUEL The fuel berth is close to the marina entrance but is tricky for a larger yacht.

REPAIRS All engineering and boatyard services are available, including rigging and sails. The capitainerie will advise.

LAUNDRY On the marina.

▼ Some charm is to be had in the old town, but be prepared for a climb

▼ There are splendid villas, which came with the 19th-century tourist invasion

Marie, close by the Hôtel de Ville (town hall) and wander the shops from there to find boutiques, souvenirs, cafés and bars (20 min walk).

Blue Beard's Chateau – **Château de Pornic** – Plage du Château (15 min walk), was built in the 10th century but got its nickname in the 15th when it was owned by Gilles de Rais, who was convicted for the serial killing of children. It is now privately owned but you can get to see the courtyard if you take one of the guided tours organised by the tourist office.

Pornic Aventure, Chemin des Trois Croix Ste Marie (40 min walk) is an adventure park set in woodland where children (and adults!) can enjoy treetop scrambling, among other things. Tuition is given, English is spoken, some families have made a complete day out of it. Zip wires, skateboards and cycles. All skills are catered for. Open Wednesday, Saturday and Sunday, 1330–1900. Booking is essential.

▲ The backstreets of Pornic are quiet and can be attractive

FOOD AND SHOPPING

● **Petit Casino** convenience store, 20 Place de L'Eglise (20 min walk).
● Fresh **bread** is available on the marina every morning, if you order in advance. There are also many **bars**, **restaurants** and **crêperies**.
● In the area close by the Hôtel de Ville you'll find fish, meat, veg and groceries mostly in small shops at quite high prices. You'll have to wander the

▶ A useful little beach close to the marina

back streets to unearth some of them. **Au Panier des Saveurs**, 11 rue de Verdun (15 min walk) is a greengrocer in this area.

● **Large supermarkets** such as E. Leclerc, Lidl, Super U et Drive and Le Marché des Saisons Pornic are all located close to each other, N of the town, beside the D213 road to Nantes (40 min walk or 10 min by taxi).

● **La Fraiseraie**, 37 Place du Petit Nice (15 min walk) is a real institution in Pornic for ice cream, jam and pasta. It started in 1970 as a strawberry-growing operation but became famous for all the tasty things that can be made out of the luscious red fruit. Find the crêperie, overlooking the river, at the foot of the castle, then discover how hard it is to get your children away from this place.

There are several enticing markets:

● The **food market** is on Wednesday and Saturday in the morning in the Birochère car park, rue de la Bernerie (40 min walk).

● The **main market** is held around the historic 17th-century covered market – Thursday and Sunday 0800–1300 (20 min walk).

● There's a **night market** every Thursday in July and August by the water. Local arts and crafts, street music, on the main road that runs alongside the marina.

FURTHER AFIELD

The train station, Place de la Gare (30 min walk, 10 min by taxi) is on the opposite bank of the river, with connections to Nantes (1 hr 8 min).

This is a convenient place to arrange a crew change with Nantes airport within reach (45 min by taxi). There are trains from Nantes to Cherbourg (approx. 5 hr) with a ferry connection to the UK, or via Paris and Eurostar to London (6.5 hr being the fastest).

There is a bus service to Nantes (2 hr).

Tourist information: Next to the railway station, Place de la Gare (30 min walk)
Web: www.en.pornic.com
Tel: +33 2 40 82 04 40

L'HERBAUDIÈRE

PORNIC 10NM, ÎLE D'YEU 20NMN, LES SABLES-D'OLONNE 40NM, PORNICHET 15NM

Welcome to the Île de Noirmoutier – not really an island because of the road bridge, but something of a small world apart from this region of France. The landscape is low-lying, the majority of the soil sandy beneath your feet. Nearly a third of the island consists of saltwater marshes created by 5th-century monks, and there are no less than 40km (25 miles) of beaches.

There is one all-tide harbour, at L'Herbaudiére on the northern tip of the island, which has no fewer than 25 bars and restaurants. There is also a harbour at Port de Morin on the W of the island, but it is shallow and largely used by local boats.

NAVIGATION

The entrance to the marina has a sharp bend so beware fishing boats that might be leaving, unseen until

▼ It's a modest marina – the main business here is fishing

▲ The salt pans cover large parts of the island

you are on top of them. Fishing boats moor to the W side of the marina. If you have any choice, avoid pontoon F, which is exposed to the early morning NE wind, the *vent solaire*, which can be troublesome. Avoid approaching a couple of hours each side of LW.

OVERVIEW
This might be good point in a lengthy cruise at which to pause for a few days. The isolation from the land makes for

a quieter and less frenetic time than in the tourist hot spots ashore. Long before tourists were the invaders, this was a Viking stronghold, which gave them power and influence throughout Brittany. They arrived around 799.

They talk of a benevolent microclimate here, naming the place 'Island of Mimosas', which flower all year round. Where there is neither salt marsh nor sand dunes, you will find evergreen oak forests. There are also fortifications from the Second World

▲ Watch for the warning signs or it's going to be a wet trip back to the mainland

▼ The causeway to the mainland, but not until LW

War, when this was part of Hitler's Atlantic Wall to protect his submarine fleets.

Before the bridge was built in 1971, the link to the mainland was via a paved sandbank that covered every high water.

The marina at L'Herbaudière was the first to be built in the Vendée in 1973. As a working port in the 17th century, it served as a base for the Loire River pilots. Fishing still thrives so expect the local catch of pollack, sea bream and striped mullet to be on the restaurant menus. Sole is highly prized here, as is line-caught sea bass. There is a fish market every day.

The marina hinterland is largely residential and Noirmoutier might be considered the 'capital' of the island – a long walk of over an hour, but 10 min by taxi. Aim for Église St Philbert and wander the narrow streets to find bakers, butchers, cafés and bars.

THINGS TO SEE AND DO
The island is heavy on scenery, beaches and atmosphere, but light on 'attractions'. You might find that is in itself the most attractive aspect of the island. The major recreations here are camping, hiking and cycling.

The nature of the light soil, fortified with seaweed, makes for perfect conditions for potato growing. If you are lucky enough to find any, try the Bonnotte potato, which was brought from Barfleur in the 1920s. It is celebrated on the first Saturday in May with a festival.

FOOD AND SHOPPING
● Marina Supermarket, 30 rue du Port, on the marina. (Note: closed 1300–1500

▲ The salt is grey (but clean) and can be found with added flavourings

daily.) Possible to arrange delivery to your boat.
● Plentiful supply of cafés, bars and restaurants on the marina.
● For large-scale shopping you will have to head to Noirmoutier – distances are from the Église St Philbert:
● Lidl, 449 rue Pierre Monnier blvd Sud (10 min walk).
● U Express, 3 rue de la Prée aux Ducs (10 min walk).

FURTHER AFIELD
There is no train service on the island, but coaches run to Nantes operated by Aléop, route 13 (1 hr 45 min).

Nantes Atlantique airport (1 hr by taxi).

Tourist information: Rue du Polder, Barbâtre (Note: this is at the far S of the island just before the bridge. The capitainerie are reported to be helpful and can probably advise you.)
Web: www.ile-noirmoutier.com/en
Tel: +33 2 51 39 80 71

▲ Port Joinville – busy in summer, but worth it if you can get a berth

ÎLE D'YEU – PORT JOINVILLE

L'HERBAUDIÈRE 20NM, **PORNICHET** 30NM, **ST GILLES-CROIX-DE-VIE** 18NM, **LES SABLES-D'OLONNE** 30NM

Only 8km (5 miles) long by 3.2km (2 miles) wide, this is an enchanting island to walk or cycle, with a secure marina in which to leave your boat. Unlike some of the other islands along this coast, it feels more detached, and far less busy than, say, Belle-Île. With its rugged coastline, beaches and dunes, it looks a picture – which might explain why artists love it so much.

NAVIGATION
This harbour on the NE side of the island, Joinville, is the only one with a marina. With sufficient rise of tide, this is a straightforward marina to enter. If it's busy, you might be met by a launch, otherwise the reception pontoon is abreast the harbour master's office. It can get full in the summer but there is an anchorage outside, although this is not good in N or E winds. Look out for speedy ferries.

OVERVIEW
This is an island that reveals its climate through the white-washed walls of its houses and the terracotta tiles on the roofs – it's beginning to feel like the Med. To see the best of the traditional architecture, head for St Sauveur, which is the island's ancient capital.

There's much history within this small island, from Neolithic markings seen on stones to the early settlements of the Irish monks who arrived from Bangor, County Down. In the 19th century, the island was hugely attractive to artists because of the sparkling quality of the light. You will see plentiful galleries and studios – Galerie Pélagie has much local art. With 300 species of birds, twitchers will enjoy this island.

THINGS TO SEE AND DO
There are many **beaches**, some nestling in rocky coves, others part of lengthy sand dunes.

Notre Dame De Bonne Nouvelle (50 min walk, 15 min cycle) overlooks the small port of La Meule. It is one of the oldest monuments on the island – dating from the 11th century.

Vieux Château (50 min walk, 15 min cycle) – this castle is one of the oldest fortifications on the island, built to protect it from the English pirate Robert Knolles. It didn't work – he seized it in 1355 and stayed for 37 years. You'll find it standing proudly on the wilder W coast.

St Sauveur (35 min walk, 12 min cycle) offers a blend of rural charm and vibrant resort. Lots of small shops to wander among in an atmospheric narrow-street setting. Buy lamb that has grazed the salt marshes.

The **Grand Phare** lighthouse (40 min walk, 10 min cycle) was built in 1829 after numerous wrecks, then was destroyed by the Germans in the Second World War and rebuilt

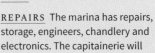

The essentials:

FUEL Fuel berth on the marina.

REPAIRS The marina has repairs, storage, engineers, chandlery and electronics. The capitainerie will direct you.

LAUNDRY Laundry and showers are below the capitainerie.

HIRE Cycle hire: cycling is the big thing here. Walk from the marina towards the town and you will find as many cycle hire shops as you could wish for.

FERRY There are frequent ferries from Fromentine – the high-speed cats taking 30 min, or 70 min by conventional ferry. Ferries also for St Gilles-Croix-de-Vie in high summer.

in 1951. It is open to visitors.

La Citadelle, rue de Pierre Levée (15 min walk, 5 min cycle) was built in the 1850s and has been a prison and barracks. It is perhaps most famous for the imprisonment of Marshal Pétain, the head of state of Vichy France, who

▼ Vieux Château – built to repel the English in the 14th century… it didn't work

was found guilty of treason in 1945.

Caval Kayak – on the beaches at Les Vieilles and Le Marais Salé (50 min walk, 12 min cycle). Watersports for children and sea kayaking (with instruction).

FOOD AND SHOPPING

- Supermarché Casino, 31 rue Calypso (7 min walk).
- Super U, rue du Nord (7 min walk).
- Épicerie Le Nav' (convenience store), 2 rue de la Plage (10 min walk).

▼ St Sauveur, where you start to get a Mediterranean feel to the place

- Boulangerie du Port, 11 rue de Marché (W side of the marina) (3 min walk).
- There is a busy quayside market daily. Apart from fish, fruit and vegetables, look out for tarte Îslaise, which is made from prunes, rum and cinnamon, traditionally served at all island weddings.
- Fishing tackle from L'Embrun, 9 Quai de la Chapelle (5 min walk).

FURTHER AFIELD

For those not cycling or walking, there is a local bus that is frequent and serves the whole island.

Tourist information: Rue du Marché, close to the W side of the marina (5 min walk)
Web: www.ile-yeu.fr
Tel: +33 2 51 58 32 58

ST GILLES-CROIX-DE-VIE

You get two resorts for the price of one here. This is a forced marriage of two towns either side of the River Vie: St Gilles-sur-Vie and Croix-de-Vie. They were joined in 1967 and are now one large resort. There are long, sandy beaches and surfing if conditions are right. It's a relaxed kind of place with no shortage of bars and restaurants, and for some reason in an otherwise rich resort, bargain clothing.

NAVIGATION

If you call ahead then you may be met by a RIB. The marina is on the W bank of the river in what was once Croix-de-Vie. You will be moored in a river with consequent fast streams. The marina can often be full, but there is a lengthy visitor pontoon beyond the marina, past the fuel berth and to port towards the bridge.

OVERVIEW

The influence of the tourist trade here is obvious in the lengthy string of apartment blocks that run for several miles along the shore, but there is still a bit of history if you hunt it down. There are two markets, which seem to thrive, and typical narrow streets lined with what were once fishermen's cottages.

They take sardines very seriously here, it being the major fishing industry. The 'Brotherhood of the

▼ The marriage of two resorts either side of the River Vie

Sardine', headed by a Grandmaster, has dedicated itself to the promotion of all things fishy in this town. A boatbuilder by the name of Beneteau was founded here in 1884 – you may have heard of him.

THINGS TO SEE AND DO

L'Atelier de la Sardine, 1 Chemin des Gabelous (20 min walk). All things sardine are covered in this museum – boats, models, history from the 17th century, photographs and sculptures and a wide variety of goodies in the

The essentials:

<u>FUEL</u> Just beyond the far end of the marina.

<u>REPAIRS</u> Chart agent, electrics, shipwrights and chandlery in the marina area.

<u>LAUNDRY</u> Behind the capitainerie.

<u>HIRE</u> Cycle hire: Roulavelo – on the marina.

▼ Sardines are the big thing here – and locals are proud of it

shop – sardine-based, of course.

Club de plage Mickey-Belugas, ave. Maurice Perray (30 min walk). A beach club for three- to 13-year-olds – games, treasure hunts, sports and swimming lessons in a heated pool.

Annual Jazz Festival – the town vibrates to the sound of jazz every year during Pentecost weekend, or Whitsuntide, which falls on the seventh Sunday after Easter. All kinds of jazz – swing, gospel, blues etc. All outdoor events are free to attend.

Surf schools, blvd des Océanides, on the Grand Plage (30 min walk).

▲ Look one way and see wide open beaches…

▶ …and look other for endless high rises

FOOD AND SHOPPING

The most varied shopping is on the same bank of the river as the marina. The opposite bank is largely residential.

- Péché Mignon, 2 rue du Général de Gaulle (10 min walk).
- SPAR (convenience store), 36 Quai de la République (5 min walk).
- Super U et Drive, 1 Imp de la Drie (20 min walk).
- Le Fournil Boulangerie Pâtisserie, 55 rue du Général de Gaulle (5 min walk).
- There is a market with plentiful local produce at Place Guy Kergoustin (4 min walk). It closes at 1300.
- Marché nocturne – an evening market with local arts and crafts, Place du Marché aux Herbes (12 min walk).
- Point Break Surf Shop, 8 Quai des Greniers (8 min walk).

FURTHER AFIELD

There is an SNCF station, Quai République (6 min walk). Trains to Nantes (1 hr 15 min) for onward connections to all parts of France.

Nearest airport at Nantes (1 hr 15 min by taxi).

Bus line 568 runs between here and Les Sables-d'Olonne, operated by Aléop.

Tourist information: Place de la Gare (6 min walk)
Web: www.payssaintgilles-tourisme.fr
Tel: +33 2 51 55 03 66

LES SABLES-D'OLONNE

▼ The colourful waterfront approach (beware the small ferry runabouts)

ÎLE DE YEU 25NM, **ST GILLES-CROIX-DE-VIE** 14NM, **LE CROISIC** 40NM, **LA ROCHELLE** 45NM

If this place is known for one thing these days, it is the Vendée Globe, the singlehanded non-stop round-the-world race for high-tech yachts, which starts from here. it has a serious resort (meaning lots of high-rise apartments) and a 3km (1.9 miles)-long beach. And it has a serious marina too – 1,500 berths – but despite the development, the town has charm.

NAVIGATION

There are two marinas here, and they are very different in atmosphere. The first on your starboard side on entering is Quai Garnier. This has only 100 berths and is often full, but it is close to some good shops, a fish market and the shoreside architecture is more interesting. But it can be noisier. This is the better place for getting easily to the town centre.

Continue to Port Olona, the larger of the two, and you'll find it quieter and much closer to chandlery, boatyard services, electrics etc. And, of course, it is the home of the Vendée boats every four years.

OVERVIEW

This was France's biggest cod-catching port in the 17th century but it has been a centre for maritime trade since it was founded in 1218. However, its prosperity predates even that by a couple of thousand years when vineyards and salt marshes were created. 'Ol-ona' means 'hill above the water' and is thought to be Celtic. During the French Revolution in the late 18th century, this was a Republican stronghold with six prisons and a guillotine.

The tourist boom developed in 1825 when the newly discovered craze for sea bathing took off, further fuelled by the advent of the railway in 1866. Then came thermal baths, the aristocracy embraced the place, and its reputation as a sophisticated resort was formed.

▼ The distinctive Tour d'Arundel in the approach channel

THINGS TO SEE AND DO

La Chaume is the oldest quarter accessible by ferry if you find yourself on the wrong side of the river. Driven by solar power, the ferry operates near the harbour mouth, Quai René Guiné. It saves a 30 min walk. La Chaume is more than worth a visit, and you'll find its character quite different to its neighbour across the river. Head for the **Place Ste Anne** to see a large mural that tells the story of the region and enjoy the narrow streets, fishermen's house and, for some reason, abundant hollyhocks. In early September, there's a **festival** of all things nautical, including fishing, sailing, sea shanties, crafts and seafoods.

Musée de l' Abbaye St-Croix, rue de Verdun (30 min walk) displays modern and contemporary art in a 17th-century Benedictine convent. The top floor is in the shape of an upturned boat's hull.

Head to **Saltworks of the Aubraie,** route de l'Aubraie (30 min walk) to see salt harvesting. There's a guided tour of the marshes by boat or on foot.

Musée du Coquillage, 8 rue du Maréchal Leclerc (20 min walk). This

The essentials:

(Note: walking times are given from Port Olona.)

FUEL Below the capitainerie in Port Olona – the reception berth is just before it.

REPAIRS 28T Travelift and all repairs are possible here.

LAUNDRY On the marina, or try Laverie Chaumoise, 60 rue du Moulin (20 min walk).

HIRE Cycle hire: Cyclotron, 66 Prom. Georges Clemenceau (25 min walk). Cyclable Les Sables-d'Olonne, 37 bis ave. François Mitterand (20 min walk).

POOL Piscine du Remblai, Prom. de l'Amiral Lafargue (25 min walk) is a heated seawater pool (goggles advised), jacuzzi and hot tubs, spa area and sunbathing.

◄ Many elegant buildings to enjoy in Les Sables

▶ 1 The pier is quite a dramatic structure; 2 The covered market is not to be missed – very good quality produce in a beautiful art deco building; 3 & 4 Don't miss L'Île Penotte – the street decorated with shells; 5 More classical elegance

shellfish museum houses 45,000 shellfish in a private collection, including starfish and sharks. There are games for children.

Zoo des Sables-d'Olonne, route du Tour de France (50 min walk) near the beach Tanchet is home to 400 species of animals, including giraffes, pandas, lions, wolves, meerkats and penguins, all living in a natural environment. There's a skatepark nearby.

Hospital Blockhaus Museum, rue de Verdun (30 min walk) is a modern building telling the story of the Second World War in a German hospital bunker that's strong on atmosphere. Tours are in English, it's family-friendly and there are games for children.

FOOD AND SHOPPING
● Head towards the beach to find the main town centre for a multitude of shops.

● Carrefour Market, rue de la Petite Garliére (12 min walk).
● Carrefour City, 7 Quai Ernest de Franqueville (nearest to Quai Garnier) (15 min walk).
● Super U et Drive, 68 rue Joseph Benatier (8 min walk).
● La Petite Boulangerie, 3 ave. Georges Pompidou (17 min walk).
● Marché des Halles Centrales, rue des Halles (20 min walk), is a daily market in a splendid market hall – oysters, crabs, fruit, veg.
● Marché de la Chaume, Place Maraud (20 min walk), was built in 1951 on the site of an old wash house. Open Tuesday to Sunday in high season from 0800–1300.

FURTHER AFIELD
There is an SNCF station, Gare des Sables-d'Olonne (20 min walk) with two trains a day to Nantes (1hr 25 min).

Bus Oléane operates 14 services around the district to campsites and different parts of town. Enquire at tourist information for the route and to buy tickets.

The nearest airport is at Nantes Atlantique (1 hr 30 min by taxi).

Tourist information: 1 Prom. Wilson (25 min walk)
Web: www.lessablesdolonne-tourisme.com
Tel: +33 2 51 96 85 85

BOURGENAY

The marina here was opened in 1985 alongside what is now a 'holiday village'. Don't expect too much history or charm, but it's a safe spot to break a passage in a clean and tidy-looking place.

NAVIGATION
Shallow at places in the entrance but pretty safe an hour or so after LW. Leading lights for a night entry. Berth to starboard on the S breakwater.

OVERVIEW
The main activities are golfing, walking and camping in a place that has the distinct feeling of a created resort.

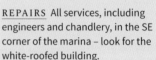

The essentials:

FUEL On the S breakwater.

REPAIRS All services, including engineers and chandlery, in the SE corner of the marina – look for the white-roofed building.

LAUNDRY Behind the capitainerie, which looks like a lighthouse.

HIRE Cycle hire: Dinovelo, Rés du Port Bourgenay (15 min walk) – tandems, child seats, electric bikes.

▼ Expect plenty of apartments like these, with not much character

▼ Not much of a traditional feel to this harbour

THINGS TO SEE AND DO

Veillon beach (25 min walk) – this is said to be one of the best beaches in the Vendée. It's 1.5km (0.9 miles) long and backed by sand dunes at the mouth of the Payre River. A sand spit across the mouth of the river has effectively created a lagoon. Lifeguards during the season. The beach is to the SE of the marina.

Aquarium de Vendée, ave. de la Mine (10 min by taxi, 40 min walk). An excursion for a wet day, perhaps. Gaze at 500 species of fish from the Atlantic, Mediterranean and Pacific oceans. There are also pony rides and a bouncy castle.

Musée Automobile de Vendée, D949 ave. des Sables (12 min by taxi ride), is a car museum with over 150 vehicles,

and has great charm. It has been in the same family for three generations.

The town of **Talmont St Hilaire** is worth a visit, offering a castle and a good market town atmosphere. The town was once a port but the sea receded and left it high and dry.

There is an amusement park,

▲ The baguette machine might be useful in the morning…

▲ …and the pizza machine later in the day

▲ The shopping is themed too, to blend in with the resort

▼ But at least the fish are real!

- A little further, on the roundabout, is **Boulangerie et Pâtisserie SORIN** (12 min walk).
- Supplies are limited here, but there is **Super U** and **Lidl** in nearby Talmont St Hilaire (10 min by taxi).

FURTHER AFIELD

The nearest train station is at Les Sables-d'Olonne, Gare des Sables-d'Olonne (35 min by taxi) with a TGV connection to Paris (approx. 3 hr 30 min).

There are bus services to Les Sables-d'Olonne (route 154) and to Talmont. Board close by the marina and the tourist information (see below) will give you the times.

La Belière Loisirs, 1088 ave. de la Plage (18 min walk on the way to Veillon beach), with trampolines, pedal cars, children's village and minigolf.

FOOD AND SHOPPING

- **Proxi Super** (small supermarket), ave. Notre Dame (10 min walk up the hill).

Tourist information: Rés du Port de Bourgenay (5 min walk)
Web: www.destination-vendeegrandlittoral.com
Tel: +33 2 51 22 23 18

ÎLE DE RÉ

(TO ST MARTIN) LES SABLES-D'OLONNE 28NM, ST GILLES-CROIX-DE-VIE
40NM, ÎLE D'YEU 51NM

If you are sailing southwards, you have now left the Vendée and entered the Charente. Île de Ré is a land of salt marshes, sand dunes, pine trees and beaches. And tourists. The villages are pretty and the sand is soft beneath your feet. Expect to be shoulder to shoulder with Parisians in high season.

There are two harbours with marinas: Ars-en-Ré is the most northerly, and St Martin-de-Ré (the island capital) is further E on the N side of the island.

▼ The marina at St Martin has a distinct feeling of being further south

NAVIGATION
There are two small basins and some careful calculation is needed here as the approach dries completely to seaward and access to the marina is via gates. Depending on draught, you may not have too much latitude either side of HW. The first you come to is the Bassin de la Criée, which is the larger of the two and will be to starboard, then further along is the Bassin de la Prée, to port, which is in the centre of the village.

OVERVIEW
Strictly speaking, it is no longer an island since a bridge was opened in

▼ Île de Ré hasn't been an island since the bridge was opened in 1988

1988. The highest point of the island is only 19m (62ft) above sea level so it's not a place for climbers; on the other hand, cyclists can enjoy flat running on 100km (62 miles) of cycle tracks. Expect to find cycle hire in almost every village.

St Martin-de-Ré is a UNESCO World Heritage site where no overhead cables are allowed and the houses can only be painted in a restricted range of colours. As a long-standing centre for the production of salt and wine, invaders have always had an eye on it. There was an English attempt in 1627, after which the fortifications surrounding St Martin were built by France's most famous military architect, Vauban.

There are three major beaches amidst many others: Plage de la Conche des Baleines (15 min cycling to the N from Ars-en-Ré) for dunes and pine forest; Les Portes-en-Ré (15 min by taxi from Ars-en-Ré); Plage de Gros Jonc (20 min cycling from St Martin), which is best for surfers, kayaks and canoes.

◀ A tourist hot spot complete with souvenirs

▼ Ars-en-Ré is a quieter, often overlooked spot

ARS-EN-RÉ

This is the quieter end of the island – a good place to see the salt pans or climb the lighthouse at Les Baleines. Close by the lighthouse is L'Arche de Noé (Noah's Ark), where you will find tropical birds and other creatures from rainforests, all in a floral setting.

Of the two marinas on the island, this will be the quieter, there being somewhat less tourist bustle here than in St Martin. Pay tribute to the church with the black-and-white spire as this provides a good landmark to show you are heading in the right direction.

▼ A donkey stands guard over the old fortifications of St Martin

▶ The church in Ars-en-Ré is a powerful landmark

The essentials:

FUEL There is a diesel pump on the E side but this may only be open to fishing boats.

CHANDLERY Blondeau Marine, 3B Quai Criée, close to the marina.

FOOD AND SHOPPING

● Large daily street **market**, Marché Ars en Ré, 12 rue du Mouillbarbe, close by the marina.

● U Express, small but well stocked, 34 rue de la Diète (12 min walk).

Tourist information: 26 Place Carnot (10 min walk), by the church
Web: www.iledere.com
Tel: +33 5 46 09 00 55

▼ You'll always find a quiet harbourside spot on the Île de Ré

ST MARTIN-EN-RÉ

This really is a place where you can step back in time to get a sense of a kind of France that you might think had disappeared. Think stone walls and cobbled streets and Vauban fortifications, but with tourists packed almost as tightly as the boats in the marina. There is great atmosphere here created by the fortifications, and much restaurant life close by – expect them to be pricey.

NAVIGATION

There is a drying entrance and you may have less than a couple of hours either side of HW to enter via lock gates. There is a waiting pontoon to starboard on the end of the Grand Mole. The bottom is very soft mud. Once through the lock, expect some tight manoeuvering.

FOOD AND SHOPPING

The major shopping is somewhat out of town toward the E, where you will find:

- Intermarché SUPER, 4 ave. des Corsaires (20 min walk).
- Lidl, 32–34 ave. Général de Gaulle (20 min walk).
- Biocoop (organic store) 17 ave. Général de Gaulle (20 min walk).

THINGS TO SEE AND DO

Donkey rides for children, Les ânes en culotte, rue Emile Atgier, to the NE of the marina (10 min walk).

FURTHER AFIELD

There are bus services from here to La Rochelle (1 hr 28 min), the bus station is at 243 Cours Vauban (10 min walk to the E of the marina).

Tourist information: 2 ave. Victor Bouthillier (6 min walk)
Web: www.iledere.com
Tel: +33 5 46 09 00 55

▲ It's not difficult to escape the summer crowds

The essentials:

FUEL There is a fuel berth, but not in the marina. Find it on the W side of the outer drying harbour.

REPAIRS All repair and chandlery services are available. Consult the capitainerie.

FACILITIES Showers in the capitainerie by the lock.

LAUNDRY In the capitainerie by the lock.

HIRE Cycle hire: La Maison Des Vélocipedes, 10 Quai de Bernonville (5 min walk); Cyclo-Surf, 55 cours Pasteur (5 min walk).

▼ When the sun has dipped, the waterfront at St Martin starts to come alive

LA ROCHELLE

LES SABLES-D'OLONNE 35NM, ÎLE D'YEU 60NM,
ST GILLES-CROIX-DE-VIE 50NM

The French rate this as being among the best cities to live in the whole of France. It's also a great place to sail to, with a totally secure harbour (the largest marina in Europe – bring your walking shoes) and lots of history and atmosphere all set in a distinctly rural landscape.

NAVIGATION

There are three marinas to choose from (and possibly another used as an overflow or for special events). None of them is cheap. Following the leading lines, the first to starboard is the largest, Port des Minimes, with over 4,000 berths, but with a longish walk to the town, although there is a waterbus. The layout of the pontoons is confusing – their website has a useful map. It's a 35 min walk from here into the old town.

Continuing upriver and passing between the two towers is the Vieux Port (or Bassin d'Échouage) which lands you as close to the town as you can possibly be. This is the place to immerse yourself in the rich atmosphere of this lively place.

The Bassin des Yachts (between the towers and then to starboard) is for larger boats or might be useful for a long stay but is not a regular haunt of visitors.

The Bassin des Chalutiers (to starboard just before the towers) is used

▼ The two famous towers mark the entrance to the inner, and more desirable harbour

largely for special events but is a good place for multihulls. You have to transit a lifting bridge.

OVERVIEW

The old part of the city has been preserved and is best seen on an evening stroll along the city walls. If walking the town, head for the unmissable Grosse Horloge clock tower and start there, being careful not the miss the streets lined with arcades that once housed merchants and moneylenders. You will find narrow streets lined with houses built from local white limestone and dating from medieval and Renaissance times.

With the safest and largest secure harbour on this coastline, La Rochelle

▼ It's an easy step ashore from the inner harbour to the heart of the city

has a rich maritime tradition dating from the Middle Ages when the city first became a free port, through the centuries of trading under sail to the New World, and now to the new deep-water port at La Pallice. Expect to come across musicians and performers on the waterfront. You might get the feeling that you have dropped into a long-running summer party.

THINGS TO SEE AND DO

(Note: walking distances from Vieux Port, which is reached from Port des Minimes by water taxi.)

There are **museums** aplenty, often with deals such as three museums for the price of two, so check at the first ticket office you visit.

The **Maritime Museum**, Place Bernard Moitessier (20 min walk). You will find this in the Vieux Port, close by the former trawler basin beyond the

---

The essentials:

FUEL 24 hr diesel at Port des Minimes by credit card on a long pontoon near the entrance.

REPAIRS For all repairs, chandlery etc head for the Zone Artisanale, which is to the E of the large marina. In the marina area, you may find nearly 100 marine businesses and it's a safe bet that one of them can help you.

FACILITIES Laundry and shower are part of the capitainerie at Port des Minimes.

HIRE Cycle hire: Greenbike La Rochelle, 41 Quai du Gabut (E side of the Vieux Port).

aquarium. One building ashore, then a trawler, weather ship and tug for you to crawl over. Signage is mostly in French. Games for children. There's a seating area if you are bringing a picnic. This is a close-up/hands-on maritime experience.

The **Natural History Museum**, 28 rue Albert 1er (15 min walk) is in the heart of the old town with botanical garden alongside. There are fossils, minerals and exhibits themed around the natural world, including a giraffe offered to King Charles X in the 19th century (closed Mondays).

Musées des Automates, 14 rue de la Désirée (10 min walk but take the waterbus across the harbour). This is a museum of moving models, including planes, cars and boats, and people – press a button to bring them to life. There's also a gigantic train set and a self-playing piano to while away a rainy afternoon. It's an old-fashioned kind of attraction, housed in two buildings. Children love it.

New World Museum, 10 rue Fleuriau (10 min walk) is a small museum telling the story of the trade between La Rochelle and North America. It's honest about France's links with the slave trade.

Aquarium, Quai Louis Prunier (15 min walk) comprises 82 aquariums and 600 species, packed with marine life. Open every day – allow 2 hr for a full visit. The audio guides are recommended. Hugely popular with families (very family friendly) so it can be crowded.

Le Bunker de la Rochelle, 8 rue des Dames (15 min walk). The bunker was built by the Germans in 1941. This is La Rochelle's wartime story – pictures, videos and exhibits with everything in English alongside the French. Small but atmospheric. Allow 1 hr.

Les Francofolies de La Rochelle musical festival takes place every year and spreads throughout the town offering everything from pop and hip-hop to all kinds of contemporary French music. Usually in mid-July.

▼ There is a great view of the city from the towers

FOOD AND SHOPPING

● Wednesday is the biggest **market** and it is held in a 19th-century building in heart of the old town close N of the Vieux Port, 1 rue Gambetta – take a plate and some bread and wander the stalls choosing what you would like to eat. Select from oysters, cheeses, paté, charcuterie and fruits.

● **Carrefour City**, 3-5 rue du Cordouan (10 min walk).

● **Carrefour City**, Place du Commandant de la Motte Rouge (7 min walk).

● **Épicerie centrale**, 19 bis rue Léonce Vieljeux (2 min walk).

● **MiniPrix** (convenience store), Quai Louis Durand (7 min walk).

● If you need charts or pilot books, then **Librairie Nautique St Nicolas** is well stocked, 61 rue St Nicolas (7 min walk).

FURTHER AFIELD

There are airports at La Rochelle, rue du Jura (12 min by taxi), with flights to Gatwick (1 hr 25 min) and other UK destinations.

Bordeaux Airport, 33700 Mérignac (2 hr taxi), flights to Gatwick (1 hr 40 min), Luton (1 hr 40 min), Manchester (1 hr 50 min) and Bristol (1 hr 35 min).

The SNCF station (imposing building with amazing clock tower) is to the SE of the Vieux Port (15 min walk). Direct train services from La Rochelle to Paris (3 hr 15 min),

and to Bordeaux (2 hr 15 min). Trains to Quimper (8 hr 34 min) and Nantes (2 hr 17 min). By making sufficient connections, it would be possible to make a crew change here via the Channel ferry ports.

If you are not visiting harbours on Île de Ré, you can get there by taking the No 11 bus from Pas des Laquais (approx. 1 hr).

Tourist information: 2 Quai Georges Simenon (8 min walk)
Web: www.larochelle-tourisme.com
Tel: +33 5 46 41 14 68

▼ Expect a rich variety of shopping, often on the expensive side

INDEX

PIC CREDITS

(Top/Bottom = T/B, Left = L)

All photography © **Paul Heiney** with the exception of the following:

Adobe Stock ©pp7, 8, 10–11, 75, 76; **Ant Bowring** © p99T; **Getty** © pp2–3, 5, 12–13, 14, 15, 16, 17, 23B, 28–9, 31T, 37, 39, 45B, 46–7, 54, 56–7, 58, 59, 60, 62, 65, 74T, 80B, 85, 86, 87, 89, 92–3, 94, 96, 98, 102–3, 114–15, 119T, 124, 125, 126, 129, 134, 135, 136, 150B, 151B, 152; **Janet Murphy** © pp63, 64, 69, 70, 71, 72, 73, 74B, 95, 97, 140, 141, 142, 143, 153, 154, 155; **Lucy Doncaster** © p52BL

Maps by **JP Map Graphics Ltd** and map data © **Eurographics**, 2022: pp6–7, 9